MEXICAN

Authentic recipes from south of the border

STERLING
New York

CONTENTS

DRINKS SNACKS AND STARTERS   4

MAINS   32

BEANS AND RICE   88

SALSAS AND SAUCES   98

SWEET TREATS   106

GLOSSARY   122

CONVERSION CHART   125

INDEX   126

DRINKS
SNACKS AND
STARTERS

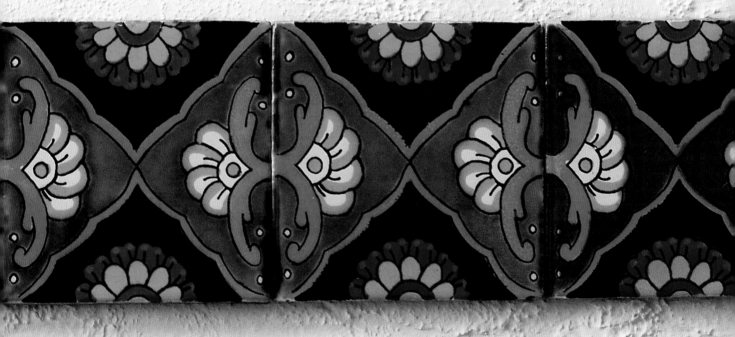

WE USED COINTREAU FOR THIS RECIPE. YOU CAN BUY SUGAR SYRUP FROM LIQUOR STORES OR MAKE YOUR OWN. STIR 1 CUP SUPERFINE SUGAR WITH 1 CUP WATER IN SMALL SAUCEPAN, OVER LOW HEAT, UNTIL SUGAR DISSOLVES; BRING TO THE BOIL. REDUCE HEAT; SIMMER, UNCOVERED, WITHOUT STIRRING, 5 MINUTES. REMOVE FROM HEAT; COOL TO ROOM TEMPERATURE. STORE IN AN AIRTIGHT CONTAINER IN THE FRIDGE FOR UP TO 1 MONTH.

2 limes, halved
1 cup ice cubes
1½ fluid ounces dark tequila
1 fluid ounce orange-flavored liqueur
1 fluid ounce sugar syrup

1 Rub cut side of one lime half around rim of 4½-fluid ounce margarita glass; turn glass upside-down and dip wet rim into saucer of salt.
2 Juice limes (you need 1 fluid ounce of juice).
3 Place ice cubes, tequila, liqueur, juice and syrup in cocktail shaker; shake vigorously. Strain into glass. Garnish with shredded lime rind made using a zester.

nutritional count per serving 0.2g total fat (0g saturated fat); 291 cal; 31.4g carbohydrate; 0.3g protein; 0.1g fiber

MARGARITA

PREP TIME 5 MINUTES ☀

frozen
MARGARITA

PREP TIME 5 MINUTES ⚙ **SERVES 1**

  2 limes, halved
1½ cups ice cubes
1½ fluid ounces dark tequila
  1 fluid ounce orange-flavored liqueur
  1 fluid ounce sugar syrup

1 Rub cut side of one lime half around rim of
4½-fluid ounce margarita glass; turn glass upside-
down and dip wet rim into saucer of salt.
2 Juice limes (you need 1 fluid ounce of juice).
3 Blend or process ingredients until smooth.
Pour into glass; garnish with fresh mint leaves
and slices of lime.

nutritional count per serving 0.2g total fat
(0g saturated fat); 291 cal; 31.4g carbohydrate;
0.3g protein; 0.1g fiber

WE USED COINTREAU FOR THIS RECIPE.
YOU CAN BUY SUGAR SYRUP FROM LIQUOR
STORES OR MAKE YOUR OWN. STIR 1 CUP
SUPERFINE SUGAR WITH 1 CUP WATER IN SMALL
SAUCEPAN, OVER LOW HEAT, UNTIL SUGAR
DISSOLVES; BRING TO THE BOIL. REDUCE HEAT;
SIMMER, UNCOVERED, WITHOUT STIRRING,
5 MINUTES. REMOVE FROM HEAT; COOL TO
ROOM TEMPERATURE. STORE IN AN AIRTIGHT
CONTAINER IN THE FRIDGE FOR UP TO 1 MONTH.

blood orange

MARGARITA

PREP TIME 5 MINUTES SERVES 1

2 limes, halved
1 cup ice cubes
1½ fluid ounces dark tequila
1 fluid ounce blood orange juice
1 fluid ounce sugar syrup

1 Rub cut side of one lime half around rim of 8½-fluid ounce old fashioned glass; turn glass upside-down and dip wet rim into saucer of salt.
2 Juice limes (you need 1 fluid ounce of juice).
3 Place ice cubes, tequila, juices and sugar syrup in cocktail shaker; shake vigorously. Strain into glass.

nutritional count per serving   2.9g total fat (1.3g saturated fat); 200 cal; 31.3g carbohydrate; 2.5g protein; 0.1g fiber

YOU CAN BUY SUGAR SYRUP FROM LIQUOR STORES OR MAKE YOUR OWN. STIR 1 CUP SUPERFINE SUGAR WITH 1 CUP WATER IN SMALL SAUCEPAN, OVER LOW HEAT, UNTIL SUGAR DISSOLVES; BRING TO THE BOIL. REDUCE HEAT; SIMMER, UNCOVERED, WITHOUT STIRRING, 5 MINUTES. REMOVE FROM HEAT; COOL TO ROOM TEMPERATURE. STORE IN AN AIRTIGHT CONTAINER IN THE FRIDGE FOR UP TO 1 MONTH.

NOT TO BE CONFUSED WITH "SANGRIA", THE SPANISH FRUIT-LACED WINE DRINK, "SANGRITA", LOOSELY MEANING "LITTLE BLOOD", IS A TANGY, SPICY AND REFRESHING DRINK TRADITIONALLY SERVED AS A CHASER OR AS AN ACCOMPANIMENT TO GOOD-QUALITY TEQUILA – ORDERED AS TEQUILA "COMPLETO". IT WAS DESIGNED TO BE SLOWLY SIPPED ALONGSIDE A SHOOTER OF TEQUILA, CUTTING THE HARSHNESS AND COOLING THE FIRE OF THE TEQUILA. MANY OF US USUALLY ASSOCIATE TEQUILA WITH THE RITUAL OF THE "SHOT" TAKEN WITH A LICK OF SALT, FINISHED WITH A WEDGE OF LIME, BUT IN REALITY, MOST TRUE TEQUILA-LOVER'S WOULD NOT DRINK TEQUILA AS A STAND-ALONE DRINK. THEY WOULD RATHER SLOWLY SIP AND SAVOR THE FLAVOR OF THE DRINK, ALONGSIDE SANGRITA TO EXTRACT THE AGAVE TASTE.

4 fluid ounces chilled tomato juice
2½ fluid ounces chilled orange juice
1½ fluid ounces lime juice
dash tabasco
pinch celery salt
pinch onion powder
4 fluid ounces tequila

1 Place juices, tabasco, celery salt and onion powder in medium jug; mix well. Pour into four 2½-fluid ounce tall shot glasses.
2 Pour tequila into four 1-fluid ounce shot glasses; serve sangrita alongside tequila shooters.

nutritional count per serving   0.4g total fat (0g saturated fat); 77 cal; 3.1g carbohydrate; 0.4g protein; 0.2g fiber

SANGRITA

PREP TIME 5 MINUTES ✸ SERVES 4

4 cups milk
2-inch strips orange rind
1 cinnamon stick
6 ounces semi-sweet chocolate,
   chopped finely

1 Bring milk, rind and cinnamon to the boil in medium saucepan. Remove from heat; stand, covered, 5 minutes.
2 Discard rind and cinnamon. Add chocolate; stir until smooth. Garnish with extra finely grated semi-sweet chocolate.

nutritional count per serving   15.3g total fat (9.5g saturated fat); 271 cal; 27.4g carbohydrate; 7.2g protein; 0.4g fiber

mexican hot
CHOCOLATE

PREP + COOK TIME 15 MINUTES (+ STANDING) ✸ **SERVES 6**

MEXICAN COFFEE

PREP + COOK TIME 15 MINUTES   SERVES 6

6 cups water

2-inch strips orange rind

½ cup coarsely ground coffee beans

¼ cup raw sugar

¼ cup firmly packed light brown sugar

1 cinnamon stick

6 cloves

1 Bring 5 cups of the water to the boil in medium saucepan; stir in rind, coffee, sugars, cinnamon and cloves. Reduce heat; simmer, uncovered, 5 minutes. Remove from heat, add remaining water; stand, covered, 5 minutes.

2 Strain mixture into large heatproof pitcher; pour into coffee cups to serve.

nutritional count per serving   0g total fat (0g saturated fat); 71 cal; 18.5g carbohydrate; 0.1g protein; 0.1g fiber

shredded pork and
BEAN SOUP

PREP + COOK TIME 2 HOURS 55 MINUTES ⊙ SERVES 6

1 large carrot, chopped coarsely
1 stalk celery, trimmed, chopped coarsely
5 cloves garlic, unpeeled, bruised
6 black peppercorns
3 sprigs fresh oregano
1 dried bay leaf
2-pound piece pork neck
8 cups chicken stock
8 cups water
1 tablespoon olive oil
1 large red onion, chopped coarsely
1 medium red bell pepper, chopped coarsely
1 medium yellow bell pepper, chopped coarsely
2 fresh long red chilies, sliced thinly
2 cloves garlic, crushed
1½ pounds canned crushed tomatoes
1 teaspoon ground cumin
2 tablespoons coarsely chopped fresh oregano
13 ounces canned kidney beans, drained, rinsed

1 Place carrot, celery, bruised garlic, peppercorns, oregano sprigs, bay leaf, pork, stock and the water in large saucepan; bring to the boil. Reduce heat; simmer, covered, 1 hour. Uncover; simmer 1 hour.
2 Transfer pork to medium bowl; using two forks, shred pork coarsely. Strain broth through muslin-lined sieve or colander into large heatproof bowl; discard solids.
3 Heat oil in same cleaned pan; cook onion, bell peppers, chili and crushed garlic, stirring, until vegetables soften.
4 Return pork and broth to pan with undrained tomatoes, cumin and chopped oregano; bring to the boil. Reduce heat; simmer, covered, 15 minutes. Add beans; simmer, covered, until soup is hot. Season to taste.

nutritional count per serving 7.4g total fat (1.6g saturated fat); 356 cal; 20.8g carbohydrate; 46.5g protein; 9.1g fiber

chipotle beef
TOSTADITAS

PREP + COOK TIME 55 MINUTES (+ STANDING) ⬡ MAKES 36

2 chipotle chilies
½ cup boiling water
6¾-inch round white corn tortillas
vegetable oil, for deep-frying
1 tablespoon vegetable oil, extra
1 small yellow onion, sliced thinly
1 clove garlic, crushed
9 ounces ground beef
1 tablespoon tomato paste
1 cup beer
¼ cup coarsely chopped fresh cilantro
½ cup sour cream

1 Cover chilies with the boiling water in small heatproof bowl; stand 20 minutes.
2 Meanwhile, cut three 2¾-inch rounds from each tortilla. Heat oil in wok; deep-fry rounds, in batches, until browned lightly. Drain on absorbent paper.
3 Drain chilies over small bowl; reserve liquid. Remove stems from chilies; discard stems. Blend or process chilies and reserved liquid until smooth.
4 Heat extra vegetable oil in medium frying pan; cook onion, stirring, until softened. Add garlic and beef; cook, stirring, until beef is changed in color. Stir in paste, beer and chili puree; bring to the boil. Reduce heat; simmer, uncovered, about 15 minutes or until liquid is almost evaporated. Stir in cilantro. Season to taste.
5 Top each tortilla crisp with rounded teaspoon of the chipotle beef then with ½ teaspoon of the sour cream.

nutritional count per piece 3.2g total fat (1.3g saturated fat); 57 cal; 4.3g carbohydrate; 2.4g protein; 0.6g fiber

fried oysters
WITH SALSA

PREP + COOK TIME 35 MINUTES ✸ **MAKES 12**

1   small tomato, chopped finely
½   medium yellow bell pepper, chopped finely
½   medium red onion, chopped finely
1   tablespoon finely chopped fresh cilantro
1   tablespoon olive oil
1   tablespoon lime juice
1   fresh small red thai (serrano) chili, seeded,
    chopped finely
12   oysters on the half shell
½   cup polenta
⅓   cup milk
1   egg, beaten lightly
pinch cayenne pepper
vegetable oil, for deep-frying

1 Preheat oven to 350°F.
2 Combine tomato, bell pepper, onion, cilantro, olive oil, juice and chili in small bowl; season to taste.
3 Remove oysters from shells; reserve oysters. Place shells on oven tray; heat in oven 5 minutes.
4 Meanwhile, combine polenta, milk, egg and pepper in small bowl.
5 Heat vegetable oil in medium saucepan. Dip oysters in batter; deep-fry oysters, in batches, until browned lightly. Drain on absorbent paper. Return oysters to shells; top with salsa.

nutritional count per oyster 5.5g total fat (1g saturated fat); 66 cal; 6.1g carbohydrate; 2.9g protein; 0.5g fiber

2 pounds skinless redfish fillets

1½ cups lime juice

¼ cup pickled sliced jalapeño chilies, drained

¼ cup olive oil

8 ounces mixed baby tomatoes, chopped coarsely

¼ cup finely chopped fresh cilantro

1 small red onion, sliced thinly

1 clove garlic, crushed

1 Remove any remaining skin or bones from fish; cut fish into 1-inch pieces.
2 Combine fish and juice in non-reactive large bowl. Cover; refrigerate overnight.
3 Drain fish; discard juice. Return fish to bowl, add remaining ingredients; toss gently to combine. Cover; refrigerate 1 hour. Season to taste.

nutritional count per serving 18.5g total fat (3.4g saturated fat); 403 cal; 4g carbohydrate; 52.5g protein; 1.9g fiber

CEVICHE, PRONOUNCED SE-VEE-CHAY, IS A LATIN-AMERICAN SPECIALTY. YOU NEED ABOUT 10 LIMES FOR THIS RECIPE. THE LIME JUICE "COOKS" THE FISH. FISH MUST BE MARINATED WITH THE LIME JUICE IN A NON-REACTIVE BOWL (ONE MADE FROM GLAZED PORCELAIN OR GLASS IS BEST), TO AVOID THE METALLIC TASTE THAT CAN RESULT IF MARINATING TAKES PLACE IN A STAINLESS-STEEL OR AN ALUMINIUM BOWL. ENSURE ALL OF THE FISH IS COMPLETELY COVERED WITH JUICE.

CEVICHE

PREP TIME 15 MINUTES (+ REFRIGERATION) ✦ SERVES 4

chili
CON QUESO

PREP + COOK TIME 20 MINUTES **MAKES 2 CUPS**

2 teaspoons vegetable oil
½ small green bell pepper, chopped finely
½ small yellow onion, chopped finely
1 tablespoon pickled sliced jalapeño chilies, drained, chopped finely
1 clove garlic, crushed
6½ ounces canned chopped tomatoes
8 ounces cream cheese, softened

1 Heat oil in medium saucepan; cook bell pepper, onion, chili and garlic, stirring, until onion softens. Add undrained tomatoes; cook, stirring, 2 minutes.
2 Add cheese; whisk until cheese melts and dip is smooth. Season to taste.
3 Serve hot with corn chips.

nutritional count per tablespoon 3.9g total fat (2.3g saturated fat); 41 cal; 0.7g carbohydrate; 1g protein; 0.2g fiber

shredded pork
CHIMICHANGA

PREP + COOK TIME 1 HOUR 50 MINUTES (+ COOLING) ✺ **SERVES 8**

1 pound diced pork
3 cloves garlic, peeled
2 black peppercorns
1 teaspoon ground cumin
3 cups water
½ cup coarsely chopped fresh cilantro
1 small red onion, chopped finely
2 fresh green jalapeño chilies, seeded, chopped finely
8 8-inch flour tortillas
vegetable oil, for deep-frying

1 Place pork, garlic, peppercorns, cumin and the water in large saucepan; bring to the boil. Reduce heat; simmer, covered, about 1 hour or until pork is tender. Cool.

2 Drain liquid from pork; discard peppercorns and liquid. Shred pork and garlic, using two forks. Combine pork mixture with cilantro, onion and chili in large bowl; season.

3 Heat tortillas according to instructions on packet. Divide pork mixture evenly between tortillas. Roll tortillas up firmly, secure with toothpick at each end of roll.

4 Heat oil in wok or large frying pan; deep-fry tortilla rolls, in batches, until browned lightly. Drain on absorbent paper. Remove toothpicks.

5 Cut each chimichanga in half; serve with guacamole (see page 105).

nutritional count per serving 13.3g total fat (2.9g saturated fat); 260 cal; 18.2g carbohydrate; 16.4g protein; 1.3g fiber

tortilla
LIME SOUP

PREP + COOK TIME 50 MINUTES ⊙ SERVES 4

1   medium white onion, chopped coarsely
2   cloves garlic, quartered
1   fresh long red chili, chopped coarsely
4   medium tomatoes, peeled, quartered
1   tablespoon peanut oil
¼   teaspoon ground allspice
1½ cups chicken stock
5   cups water
2   teaspoons finely grated lime rind
¼   cup lime juice
¼   cup tomato paste
⅓   cup peanut oil, extra
6   6-inch corn tortillas, cut into ¾-inch wide strips
1   medium avocado, chopped finely
2   scallions, chopped finely
¼   cup coarsely chopped fresh cilantro

1 Blend or process white onion, garlic, chili and tomato until smooth.

2 Heat oil in large saucepan; cook tomato mixture and allspice, stirring, until fragrant.

3 Add stock, the water, rind, juice and paste; bring to the boil. Reduce heat; simmer, uncovered, about 15 minutes or until soup thickens. Season to taste.

4 Meanwhile, heat extra oil in medium frying pan; cook tortilla strips in batches, until golden. Drain on absorbent paper.

5 Divide tortilla strips into bowls; ladle soup over. Serve topped with combined avocado, scallions and cilantro.

nutritional count per serving 33.8g total fat (6.5g saturated fat); 422 cal; 20.6g carbohydrate; 6.4g protein; 5.7g fiber

pork, olive and egg
EMPANADAS

PREP + COOK TIME 1 HOUR ✦ **MAKES 24**

1 tablespoon olive oil

1 medium yellow onion, chopped finely

½ teaspoon each ground cumin, ground cinnamon and smoked paprika

¼ teaspoon each ground nutmeg and ground cloves

12 ounces ground pork

2 hard-boiled eggs, grated coarsely

⅓ cup pitted black olives, chopped finely

6 sheets shortcrust pastry

1 egg, beaten lightly

1 Heat oil in large frying pan; cook onion, stirring, until soft. Add spices and pork; cook, stirring, until browned. Cool.

2 Stir hard-boiled eggs and olives into pork mixture; season to taste.

3 Preheat oven to 400°F. Oil two oven trays.

4 To make empanadas, cut 5-inch rounds from pastry. Drop heaped tablespoons of filling onto rounds; brush edges with beaten egg. Fold rounds in half to enclose filling; pinch edges to seal.

5 Place empanadas on oven trays with sealed edge upright; brush with egg.

6 Bake empanadas about 25 minutes or until browned lightly. Serve with lemon wedges, if you like.

nutritional count per empanada 14g total fat (6.7g saturated fat); 230 cal; 19.2g carbohydrate; 6.7g protein; 0.9g fiber

1½ pounds canned kidney beans, drained, rinsed

⅓ cup chunky tomato salsa

⅓ cup finely chopped fresh cilantro

7 ounces corn chips

1½ cups coarsely grated cheddar cheese

2 cups finely shredded iceberg lettuce

1 small tomato, chopped coarsely

½ small avocado, chopped coarsely

2 tablespoons lime juice

1 Preheat oven to 425°F.

2 Combine half the beans with salsa; mash until chunky. Stir in remaining beans and cilantro.

3 Spread half the chips in medium shallow baking dish; top with half the cheese and half the bean mixture. Top with remaining chips, remaining cheese then remaining bean mixture. Cook 10 minutes.

4 Place lettuce, tomato and avocado in medium bowl with juice; toss gently to combine. Season to taste.

5 Serve nachos topped with salad.

nutritional count per serving 24.5g total fat (11.6g saturated fat); 444 cal; 33.7g carbohydrate; 17.3g protein; 10.8g fiber

BEAN NACHOS

PREP + COOK TIME 20 MINUTES ✦ SERVES 6

crab
TOSTADAS

PREP + COOK TIME 25 MINUTES ⬡ SERVES 4

vegetable oil, for shallow-frying
4   6-inch flour tortillas
13   ounces canned kidney beans, drained,
     rinsed, mashed
½   cup pitted black olives
1   cup coarsely grated cheddar cheese
1   medium tomato, sliced thinly
1½   cups shredded iceberg lettuce
5½   ounces fresh cooked crab meat

AVOCADO CREAM

2   medium avocados, chopped coarsely
2   tablespoons lime juice
½   cup sour cream
2   scallions, sliced thinly
1½   tablespoons finely chopped fresh cilantro

1 Make avocado cream.
2 Heat oil in medium frying pan; shallow-fry tortillas, one at a time, until browned both sides and crisp. Drain on absorbent paper.
3 Spread tortillas with avocado cream then mashed beans; top with olives, cheese, tomato, lettuce and crab meat. Season with freshly ground black pepper.

AVOCADO CREAM Mash avocado with juice and sour cream in medium bowl with fork until well combined; stir in scallions and cilantro. Season to taste.

nutritional count per serving 44.9g total fat (19.1g saturated fat); 611 cal; 26.3g carbohydrate; 22.4g protein; 7.5g fiber

NAMED AFTER CAESAR CARDINI, THE ITALIAN-AMERICAN WHO TOSSED THE FIRST CAESAR IN MEXICO DURING THE 1920s, THIS SALAD ALWAYS CONTAINS FRESH CROUTONS, CRISP ROMAINE LETTUCE LEAVES, LIGHTLY BOILED EGGS, LEMON JUICE, OLIVE OIL, WORCESTERSHIRE SAUCE AND PARMESAN CHEESE BUT NO ONE INGREDIENT SHOULD DOMINATE.

classic
CAESAR SALAD

PREP + COOK TIME 45 MINUTES ⬙ SERVES 4

½ loaf ciabatta
1 clove garlic, crushed
⅓ cup olive oil
2 eggs
3 baby romaine lettuces, leaves separated
1 cup flaked parmesan cheese

CAESAR DRESSING

1 clove garlic, crushed
1 tablespoon dijon mustard
2 tablespoons lemon juice
2 teaspoons worcestershire sauce
2 tablespoons olive oil

1 Preheat oven to 350°F.
2 Cut bread into ¾-inch cubes; combine garlic and oil in large bowl with bread. Toast bread on oven tray until croûtons are browned.
3 Make caesar dressing.
4 Bring water to the boil in small saucepan, add eggs; cover pan tightly, remove from heat. Remove eggs from water after 2 minutes. When cool enough to handle, break eggs into large bowl; add lettuce, mixing gently so egg coats leaves.
5 Add cheese, croûtons and dressing to bowl; toss gently to combine. Season to taste.

CAESAR DRESSING Place ingredients in screw-top jar; shake well.

nutritional count per serving 39.1g total fat (9.1g saturated fat); 566 cal; 33.1g carbohydrate; 18.4g protein; 5.6g fiber

THIS IS OUR VERSION OF HUEVOS RANCHEROS, OR RANCH-STYLE EGGS, WHICH TRADITIONALLY IS MADE WITH FRIED EGGS AND BEANS. FOR AN EXTRA BITE, SERVE WITH TABASCO, A FIERY SAUCE MADE FROM HOT RED CHILIES.

scrambled eggs with
FRESH TOMATO SALSA

PREP + COOK TIME 20 MINUTES ✱ SERVES 4

3 cured chorizo sausages, sliced thickly
8 eggs
½ cup heavy cream
¾ ounce butter
4 6-inch flour tortillas
1 cup coarsely grated cheddar cheese

FRESH TOMATO SALSA

2 small tomatoes, chopped finely
½ small red onion, chopped finely
1 tablespoon red wine vinegar
1 tablespoon olive oil
¼ cup coarsely chopped fresh cilantro

1 Preheat oven to 325°F.
2 Make fresh tomato salsa.
3 Cook chorizo on heated oiled grill plate (or grill or barbecue) until well browned. Drain on paper towel; cover to keep warm.
4 Whisk eggs and cream in medium bowl. Melt butter in medium frying pan; cook egg mixture over low heat, stirring gently, until creamy.
5 Meanwhile, place tortillas on oven tray, sprinkle with cheese; warm in oven until cheese melts.
6 Divide tortillas between serving plates; top with egg, chorizo and salsa.

FRESH TOMATO SALSA Combine tomatoes, onion, vinegar and oil in small bowl. Cover; stand 15 minutes. Stir in cilantro just before serving; season to taste.

nutritional count per serving · 81.7g total fat (35.8g saturated fat); 987 cal; 16.2g carbohydrate; 48.2g protein; 1.9g fiber

MAINS

fish
BURRITOS

PREP + COOK TIME 30 MINUTES (+ REFRIGERATION) ✸ MAKES 8

1 cup coarsely chopped fresh cilantro

2 teaspoons finely chopped cilantro root and stem mixture

1 fresh long red chili, chopped coarsely

1 clove garlic, quartered

1½ teaspoons sweet paprika

1 teaspoon ground cumin

⅓ cup olive oil

1½ ounces small white fish fillets, halved

8 8-inch flour tortillas

1 baby romaine lettuce, leaves separated

1 lebanese cucumber, sliced thinly

LIME BUTTERMILK DRESSING

¼ cup buttermilk

1 teaspoon finely grated lime rind

2 teaspoons lime juice

1 Blend or process chopped cilantro, root and stem mixture, chili, garlic, spices and ¼ cup of the oil until smooth. Combine cilantro mixture and fish in large bowl. Cover; refrigerate 30 minutes.

2 Meanwhile, make lime buttermilk dressing.

3 Heat remaining oil in large frying pan; cook fish, in batches, until browned both sides and cooked through. Cover to keep warm.

4 Meanwhile, heat tortillas according to instructions on packet.

5 Divide lettuce, cucumber, fish and dressing, between tortillas; wrap to enclose filling.

LIME BUTTERMILK DRESSING Combine ingredients in small pitcher; season to taste.

nutritional count per burrito 14g total fat (2.5g saturated fat); 303 cal; 19g carbohydrate; 24.3g protein; 2g fiber

chili seared tuna with avocado cream
AND GRILLED CORN

PREP + COOK TIME 1 HOUR (+ STANDING & REFRIGERATION) ⚙ SERVES 4

4   chipotle chilies
1   tablespoon olive oil
1   small yellow onion, chopped finely
2   cloves garlic, crushed
⅓   cup loosely packed fresh oregano leaves
2   tablespoons tomato paste
2   tablespoons water
4   6½-ounce tuna steaks
2   trimmed corn cobs
8   8-inch flour tortillas
2   limes, cut into wedges

AVOCADO CREAM

2   small avocados, chopped coarsely
½   cup sour cream
¼   cup coarsely chopped fresh cilantro
1   tablespoon lime juice

1 Cover chilies with boiling water in small heatproof bowl; stand 20 minutes Drain chilies; discard stems, chop chilies coarsely.

2 Heat oil in small frying pan; cook onion and garlic, stirring, until onion softens. Stir in chili, oregano, paste and the water; bring to the boil. Remove from heat; blend or process mixture, pulsing, until mixture forms thick paste.

3 Place fish, in single layer, in large shallow dish; using fingers, pat chili paste onto both sides of fish. Cover; refrigerate 30 minutes.

4 Meanwhile, make avocado cream.

5 Cook corn on heated oiled grill plate (or grill or barbecue) until browned lightly and just tender. Remove from heat; slice thickly, cover to keep warm.

6 Cook undrained fish on same heated oiled grill plate until cooked as desired. Cover; stand 5 minutes. Slice fish thickly.

7 Meanwhile, heat tortillas according to instructions on packet.

8 Divide fish, corn, avocado cream and tortillas between serving plates. Serve with lime wedges.

AVOCADO CREAM Blend or process avocado and sour cream until smooth; stir in cilantro and juice. Season to taste.

nutritional count per serving 49.6g total fat (17.5g saturated fat); 929 cal; 53.8g carbohydrate; 62.7g protein; 8.4g fiber

CEVICHE, PRONOUNCED SE-VEE-CHAY, IS A LATIN-AMERICAN SPECIALTY.
THE ACIDS IN THE CITRUS MARINADE SLIGHTLY COOK THE VERY THINLY SLICED
RAW SEAFOOD. USE THE FRESHEST, SASHIMI-QUALITY FISH YOU CAN FIND.
RAW FISH SOLD AS SASHIMI HAS TO MEET STRINGENT GUIDELINES REGARDING
ITS HANDLING AND TREATMENT AFTER LEAVING THE WATER. WE SUGGEST YOU
SEEK LOCAL ADVICE FROM AUTHORITIES BEFORE EATING ANY RAW SEAFOOD.

salmon
CEVICHE SALAD

PREP TIME 25 MINUTES ✸ **SERVES 4**

2 medium oranges
12½-ounce piece sashimi-quality salmon, sliced thinly
5½ ounces watercress, trimmed

ORANGE AND DILL DRESSING

1 tablespoon white wine vinegar
1 tablespoon drained baby capers, rinsed
2 teaspoons finely chopped fresh dill

1 Segment oranges over small bowl; reserve ¼ cup orange juice for the dressing.
2 Make orange and dill dressing.
3 Combine salmon and half the dressing in medium bowl; stand 5 minutes.
4 Place salmon mixture in large serving bowl with remaining dressing, watercress and orange segments; toss gently to combine. Season to taste.

ORANGE AND DILL DRESSING Place vinegar, capers, dill and reserved juice in screw-top jar; shake well.

nutritional count per serving 7.3g total fat (1.6g saturated fat); 185 cal; 7.4g carbohydrate; 21g protein; 2.6g fiber

SOAK UNSHUCKED EARS OF CORN IN A PAN OF COLD WATER FOR AN HOUR OR SO. PULL BACK EACH EAR'S HUSK WITHOUT REMOVING IT THEN REMOVE THE SILK. BRUSH MELTED BUTTER OVER THE KERNELS THEN RE-COVER EAR WITH THE HUSK. PUT CORN DIRECTLY ON YOUR HOT BARBECUE GRILL FOR ABOUT 10 MINUTES, TURNING ONCE. THE RESULT IS DELICIOUS.

char-grilled scallops with
CORN SALSA

PREP + COOK TIME 45 MINUTES (+ REFRIGERATION) ✪ **SERVES 4**

36 scallops, roe removed
2 cloves garlic, crushed
2 tablespoons lime juice
1 tablespoon olive oil
2 corn cobs, trimmed
6½ ounces grape tomatoes, halved
1 large avocado, chopped coarsely
1 medium red onion, chopped finely
1 medium green bell pepper, chopped finely
2 fresh small red thai (serrano) chilies, chopped finely
¼ cup coarsely chopped fresh cilantro
8 6-inch white corn tortillas
2 limes, cut into wedges

LIME DRESSING

¼ cup lime juice
½ teaspoon ground cumin
2 teaspoons olive oil

1 Combine scallops, garlic, juice and oil in large bowl. Cover; refrigerate 3 hours or overnight.
2 Make lime dressing.
3 Cook corn on heated oiled grill plate (or grill or barbecue) until browned lightly and just tender. Using sharp knife, cut corn kernels from cobs. Combine corn kernels in large bowl with tomato, avocado, onion, bell pepper, chili, cilantro and dressing; season to taste.
4 Cook drained scallops, in batches, on same heated grill plate until browned lightly and cooked as desired. Remove from heat; cover to keep warm.
5 Using tongs, place tortillas, one at a time, briefly, on same grill plate to lightly brown both sides (work quickly as tortillas toughen if overcooked). Wrap tortillas in tea towel to keep warm.
6 Serve scallops with salsa, tortillas and lime wedges.

LIME DRESSING Place ingredients in screw-top jar; shake well.

nutritional count per serving 24.1g total fat (4.4g saturated fat); 578 cal; 50.6g carbohydrate; 37.8g protein; 12.2g fiber

1 tablespoon olive oil
1 pound ground beef
1 medium yellow onion, chopped finely
1 clove garlic, crushed
1 teaspoon ground cumin
¼ teaspoon chili powder
12½ ounces canned crushed tomatoes
½ cup water
13 ounces canned kidney beans, drained, rinsed
4 8-inch flour tortillas
1 cup coarsely grated cheddar cheese
1 teaspoon hot paprika
¾ cup sour cream
¼ cup fresh cilantro leaves

1 Heat oil in medium frying pan; cook beef, stirring, until browned. Add onion, garlic, cumin and chili powder; cook, stirring, until onion softens. Stir in undrained tomatoes, the water and beans; simmer, uncovered, about 15 minutes or until mixture thickens. Remove from heat; season to taste.
2 Preheat oven to 400°F.
3 Divide warm beef filling between tortillas, roll to enclose filling; secure with toothpicks.
4 Place filled tortillas on oiled oven tray; sprinkle with cheese and paprika.
5 Bake burritos about 10 minutes or until heated through. Remove toothpicks; serve topped with sour cream, cilantro and, if you like, guacamole (see page 105).

nutritional count per burrito 45g total fat (24g saturated fat); 723 cal; 34.1g carbohydrate; 42.4g protein; 7.3g fiber

beef
BURRITOS

PREP + COOK TIME 55 MINUTES ✦ MAKES 4

pork and cheese
QUESADILLAS

PREP + COOK TIME 50 MINUTES ✹ SERVES 4

1 tablespoon olive oil
1 pound ground pork
1 medium green bell pepper, chopped finely
1 fresh long red chili, chopped finely
1 clove garlic, crushed
½ cup coarsely chopped fresh cilantro
8 8-inch flour tortillas
2 tablespoons olive oil, extra
2 cups coarsely grated cheddar cheese

1 Heat oil in large frying pan; cook pork, stirring, until browned. Add green bell pepper, chili and garlic; cook, stirring, until fragrant. Remove from heat; stir in cilantro, season to taste.
2 Brush one side of each tortilla with extra oil. Spread pork mixture evenly over half the tortillas, oiled side down; sprinkle with cheese. Top with remaining tortillas, oiled side up.
3 Cook quesadillas, in batches, in heated sandwich press or frying pan until browned lightly. Cut quesadillas into quarters; serve with guacamole (see page 105), if you like.

nutritional count per serving 47.5g total fat (19g saturated fat); 763 cal; 36.3g carbohydrate; 46.8g protein; 2.7g fiber

chicken
ENCHILADAS

PREP + COOK TIME 1 HOUR 25 MINUTES ⊛ MAKES 10

3   chipotle chilies
1   cup boiling water
1   pound chicken breast fillets
1   tablespoon vegetable oil
1   large red onion, chopped finely
2   cloves garlic, crushed
1   teaspoon ground cumin
1   tablespoon tomato paste
1½   pound canned crushed tomatoes
1   tablespoon finely chopped fresh oregano
⅔   cup sour cream
1½   cups coarsely grated cheddar cheese
10   6-inch flour tortillas

1 Cover chilies with the boiling water in small heatproof bowl; stand 20 minutes. Discard stems from chilies. Blend or process chilies with soaking liquid until smooth.

2 Meanwhile, place chicken in medium saucepan of boiling water; return to the boil. Reduce heat; simmer, covered, about 10 minutes or until chicken is cooked through. Remove chicken from poaching liquid; cool 10 minutes. Discard poaching liquid (or keep for another use); shred chicken finely.

3 Preheat oven to 350°F. Oil shallow rectangular 12-cup ovenproof dish.

4 Heat oil in large frying pan; cook onion, stirring, until softened. Reserve half of the onion in small bowl.

5 Add garlic and cumin to remaining onion in pan; cook, stirring, until fragrant. Add chili mixture, tomato paste, undrained tomatoes and oregano; bring to the boil. Reduce heat; simmer, uncovered, 1 minute. Remove sauce from heat. Season to taste.

6 Meanwhile, combine shredded chicken, reserved onion, half the sour cream and a third of the cheese in medium bowl.

7 Heat tortillas according to instructions on packet. Dip tortillas, one at a time, in tomato sauce in pan; place on board. Place ¼ cup of the chicken mixture along edge of each tortilla; roll enchiladas to enclose filling.

8 Spread ½ cup tomato sauce into dish. Place enchiladas, seam-side down, in dish (they should fit snugly, without overcrowding). Pour remaining tomato sauce over enchiladas; sprinkle with remaining cheese.

9 Cook enchiladas, in oven, uncovered, about 15 minutes or until cheese melts and enchiladas are heated through. Serve with remaining sour cream; sprinkle with cilantro leaves, if you like.

nutritional count per enchilada   9.4g total fat (9.4g saturated fat); 381 cal; 29.4g carbohydrate; 22g protein; 3.1g fiber

SALTED COD, ALSO CALLED SALT COD, BACCALA, BACALHAU,
BACALAO AND MORUE, IS AVAILABLE FROM ITALIAN, SPANISH AND
PORTUGUESE DELICATESSENS AND SOME SPECIALTY FOOD STORES.
IT NEEDS TO BE DE-SALTED AND REHYDRATED BEFORE USE.

salt cod with
ROASTED TOMATOES

PREP + COOK TIME 50 MINUTES (+ REFRIGERATION & STANDING) **SERVES 6**

3   pounds salted cod fillets, skin on
6   large tomatoes
½   cup olive oil
1   medium yellow onion, chopped coarsely
2   ancho chilies
¼   cup boiling water
1   pound baby new potatoes, halved
4   medium yellow onions, chopped finely
6   cloves garlic, crushed
1   teaspoon smoked paprika
1   cup pimiento-stuffed green olives
½   cup coarsely chopped fresh flat-leaf parsley

1 Rinse fish under cold water to remove excess salt.
Place fish in large bowl, cover with cold water;
refrigerate, covered, overnight, changing the water
three or four times. Drain fish; discard water.
2 Preheat oven to 400°F.
3 Remove cores from tops of tomatoes; cut a small
cross in the skin at base of each tomato. Place on
oiled oven tray, drizzle with 1 tablespoon of the oil;
roast 15 minutes or until tomatoes begin to soften.
When cool enough to handle, peel away skins.

4 Meanwhile, place fish in large saucepan with
coarsely chopped onion, cover with water; bring
to the boil. Reduce heat; simmer, uncovered,
15 minutes or until fish is cooked. Drain fish;
discard liquid and onion. Remove skin and bones
from fish; flake fish into 1½-inch pieces.
5 Cover chilies with the boiling water in small
heatproof bowl; stand 20 minutes. Drain chilies;
discard stems and seeds, chop chilies coarsely.
Blend or process tomatoes and chilies until smooth.
6 Boil, steam or microwave potatoes until tender;
drain.
7 Heat remaining oil in large frying pan; cook
finely chopped onion and garlic, stirring, until
onion is softened and browned lightly. Add paprika;
cook, stirring, 1 minute. Add tomato mixture,
fish, potatoes, olives and parsley; season to taste,
stir gently until heated through.

nutritional count per serving   3.8g total fat
(0.6g saturated fat); 141 cal; 3.1g carbohydrate;
22.7g protein; 1.2g fiber

SERVING SUGGESTION
Serve with crusty bread to mop up
the juices, steamed green beans
and rice or a green salad.

CHICKEN MOLE

PREP + COOK TIME 1 HOUR 20 MINUTES ✪ SERVES 6

6 1-pound small chickens
⅓ cup all-purpose flour
¼ cup olive oil
1 medium yellow onion, chopped finely
2 cloves garlic, crushed
1 cinnamon stick
½ teaspoon ground nutmeg
¼ teaspoon ground cloves
1½ pounds canned crushed tomatoes
1 large red bell pepper, sliced thinly
1 cup dry white wine
2 ounces semi-sweet chocolate, chopped finely
⅓ cup coarsely chopped fresh flat-leaf parsley

1 Rinse chickens under cold water; pat dry with absorbent paper. Using kitchen scissors, cut along sides of chickens' backbones; discard backbones. Halve chickens along breastbones then cut each half into two pieces.
2 Coat chicken in flour; shake off excess. Heat oil in large frying pan; cook chicken, in batches, until browned. Drain on absorbent paper.
3 Cook onion and garlic in same pan, stirring, until onion softens. Add spices; cook, stirring, until fragrant.
4 Return chicken to pan with undrained tomatoes, bell pepper and wine; simmer, covered, 20 minutes. Uncover; simmer about 20 minutes or until chicken is tender and sauce thickens slightly. Add chocolate; cook, stirring, until smooth. Discard cinnamon stick; season to taste. Serve chicken with sauce; sprinkle with parsley.

nutritional count per serving 51.9g total fat (15.3g saturated fat); 788 cal; 20.1g carbohydrate; 52.8g protein; 3.3g fiber

marinated
CHILI CHICKENS

PREP + COOK TIME 1 HOUR 20 MINUTES (+ REFRIGERATION) ✦ SERVES 8

4   1-pound small chickens
2   small yellow onions, chopped coarsely
8   cloves garlic, peeled
8   fresh long red chilies
⅓   cup red wine vinegar
1   tablespoon ground cumin
2   tablespoons olive oil
4   medium ripe tomatoes, quartered

1 Rinse chickens under cold water; pat dry with absorbent paper. Using kitchen scissors, cut along sides of chickens' backbones; discard backbones. Halve chickens along breastbones.

2 Blend or process onion, garlic, chilies, vinegar and cumin until almost smooth.

3 Heat oil in large frying pan, add onion mixture; cook, stirring, until fragrant.

4 Blend or process tomatoes until smooth, add to onion mixture; cook, stirring, until mixture boils. Reduce heat; simmer, uncovered, stirring, about 20 minutes or until thickened. Season to taste. Brush chickens with half of the chili sauce; cover, refrigerate 3 hours.

5 Preheat oven to 425°F.

6 Place chickens, skin-side up, on oiled rack in large shallow baking dish; roast about 30 minutes or until cooked through.

7 Serve chicken with remaining chili sauce and, if you like, green salad leaves, and grilled corn and zucchini salsa (see page 102).

nutritional count per serving 19.3g total fat (5.1g saturated fat); 311 cal; 3.6g carbohydrate; 29.7g protein; 2g fiber

chicken in
pumpkin seed and
TOMATILLO SAUCE

PREP + COOK TIME 1 HOUR ⚙ **SERVES 6**

SERVING SUGGESTION
Serve with steamed rice,
lime wedges and fresh
cilantro leaves.

2 medium tomatoes, quartered
1 medium yellow onion, quartered
2 tablespoons olive oil
6 chicken thigh cutlets
6 chicken drumsticks
1½ cups chicken stock
1 cup pumpkin seed kernels (pepitas), roasted
2 tablespoons pickled sliced jalapeño chilies, drained
½ cup drained chopped tomatillos
2 cloves garlic, quartered
½ cup firmly packed fresh cilantro leaves
⅓ cup coarsely chopped fresh chives
½ teaspoon ground cumin

1 Preheat oven to 400°F.
2 Place tomato and onion on oiled oven tray; drizzle with half the oil. Roast, uncovered, about 25 minutes or until vegetables soften. Cool.
3 Meanwhile, place chicken in large saucepan with stock; bring to the boil. Reduce heat; simmer, covered, about 20 minutes or until chicken is just cooked through. Remove chicken from pan; reserve 1¼ cups of stock.
4 Blend or process pumpkin seed kernels until a fine powder; sift powder through fine sieve. Blend or process pumpkin seed powder with tomato and onion mixture, chili, tomatillos, garlic, cilantro, chives and cumin until smooth.
5 Heat remaining oil in same cleaned pan; cook chicken, in batches, until browned. Remove from pan. Add pumpkin seed mixture to pan; cook, stirring, 3 minutes. Add reserved stock; simmer, uncovered, 2 minutes. Return chicken to pan; simmer, uncovered, until chicken is heated through. Season to taste.

nutritional count per serving 52g total fat (13g saturated fat); 708 cal; 8.6g carbohydrate; 50.1g protein; 5g fiber

POMEGRANATE PULP CONSISTS OF THE SEEDS
AND THE EDIBLE PULP SURROUNDING THEM;
IT HAS A TANGY SWEET-SOUR FLAVOR.

chicken in almond
POMEGRANATE SAUCE

PREP + COOK TIME 35 MINUTES ⚙ **SERVES 4**

2 medium pomegranates

1½ cups water

⅓ cup firmly packed light brown sugar

2 tablespoons olive oil

4 6½-ounce chicken breast fillets

1 large yellow onion, sliced thickly

2 cloves garlic, crushed

1 tablespoon all-purpose flour

1 teaspoon each sweet paprika, ground cumin and
   ground cilantro

½ teaspoon ground cinnamon

pinch chili powder

½ cup chicken stock

⅓ cup blanched almonds, roasted

⅓ cup coarsely chopped fresh cilantro

1 Cut pomegranates in half, scoop out pulp.
Reserve about ⅓ cup pulp. Place remaining pulp
in small saucepan with the water and sugar; stir
over heat, without boiling, until sugar dissolves.
Simmer, uncovered, 5 minutes; strain syrup into
medium heatproof jug.

2 Heat half the oil in large frying pan; cook chicken,
in batches, until browned. Remove from pan.

3 Heat remaining oil in same pan; cook onion
and garlic, stirring, until onion softens. Add flour
and spices; cook, stirring, about 1 minute or until
mixture is just browned and dry. Gradually stir in
stock and pomegranate syrup; cook, stirring, until
mixture boils and thickens slightly.

4 Return chicken to pan; simmer, covered, about
5 minutes or until cooked through. Stir in reserved
pomegranate pulp, nuts and cilantro; season
to taste.

nutritional count per serving 28g total fat
(5.3g saturated fat); 566 cal; 29.3g carbohydrate;
47.8g protein; 4.8g fiber

2 tablespoons vegetable oil
1 medium yellow onion, chopped finely
1 clove garlic, crushed
1 teaspoon each ground cumin and ground cilantro
½ teaspoon chili powder
1½ pounds ground beef
1½ pounds canned crushed tomatoes
13 ounces canned mexican-style beans, drained
⅓ cup sour cream
⅓ cup loosely packed fresh cilantro leaves

1 Heat half the oil in large frying pan; cook onion, garlic and spices, stirring, until onion softens.
2 Combine beef with onion mixture in medium bowl; season. Using hands, roll level tablespoons of mixture into balls.
3 Heat remaining oil in same pan; cook meatballs, in batches, until browned all over. Remove from pan.
4 Add tomato and beans to same pan; bring to the boil. Reduce heat; simmer, uncovered, about 5 minutes or until mixture thickens slightly. Return meatballs to pan; simmer, uncovered, about 10 minutes or until meatballs are cooked through. Season to taste.
5 Serve meatballs with sour cream, cilantro and, if you like, guacamole (see page 105).

nutritional count per serving 32.2g total fat (13.4g saturated fat); 562 cal; 20.4g carbohydrate; 44.6g protein; 7.8g fiber

ALBONDIGAS

PREP + COOK TIME 50 MINUTES ✸ SERVES 4

MEATBALLS AND SAUCE CAN BE MADE A DAY AHEAD AND REFRIGERATED, COVERED SEPARATELY.

SERVING SUGGESTION
Serve with flour tortillas to scoop up the sauce.

blackened
STEAK SALAD

PREP + COOK TIME 30 MINUTES ❖ **SERVES 4**

4 6-inch flour tortillas

1-pound beef fillet

2 teaspoons hot paprika

1 teaspoon ground black pepper

½ teaspoon cayenne pepper

¼ teaspoon each dried oregano and dried thyme

3 medium tomatoes, chopped finely

1 large green bell pepper, chopped finely

1 lebanese cucumber), seeded, chopped finely

½ cup coarsely chopped fresh mint

1 tablespoon olive oil

1 tablespoon balsamic vinegar

1 clove garlic, crushed

1 lime, cut into wedges

1 Cook tortillas on heated oiled grill plate (or grill or barbecue) both sides until browned lightly. Break into coarse pieces.

2 Rub beef with combined spices, season; cook on heated oiled grill plate (or grill or barbecue), turning, until browned and cooked as desired. Cover beef; stand 5 minutes then slice thinly.

3 Place beef and tortillas pieces in large bowl with remaining ingredients; toss gently to combine, season to taste. Serve with lime wedges.

nutritional count per serving   13.7g total fat (4g saturated fat); 312 cal; 14.5g carbohydrate; 30.6g protein; 3.4g fiber

SERVING SUGGESTION
Serve with steamed rice;
top with thinly sliced white onion
and fresh cilantro leaves.

chili
CON CARNE

PREP + COOK TIME 3 HOURS 45 MINUTES (+ STANDING) ⊛ **SERVES 8**

1 cup dried kidney beans
3 pounds beef chuck steak
8 cups water
1 tablespoon olive oil
2 medium yellow onions, chopped coarsely
2 cloves garlic, crushed
2 teaspoons each ground cilantro, ground cumin and sweet paprika
½ teaspoon cayenne pepper
1½ pounds canned crushed tomatoes
2 tablespoons tomato paste
4 scallions, chopped coarsely
2 tablespoons coarsely chopped fresh cilantro
⅓ cup finely chopped pickled jalapeño chilies

1 Place beans in medium bowl, cover with water; stand overnight. Drain.

2 Place beef and the water in large saucepan; bring to the boil. Reduce heat; simmer, covered, 1½ hours.

3 Drain beef in large muslin-lined strainer over large heatproof bowl; reserve 3½ cups of the cooking liquid. Using two forks, shred beef.

4 Heat oil in same pan; cook brown onion and garlic, stirring, until onion softens. Add spices; cook, stirring, until fragrant. Add beans, undrained tomatoes, paste and 2 cups of the reserved cooking liquid; bring to the boil. Reduce heat; simmer, covered, 1 hour.

5 Add beef and remaining reserved cooking liquid to pan; simmer, covered, about 30 minutes or until beans are tender. Remove from heat; stir in scallions, cilantro and chili. Season to taste.

nutritional count per serving 11.5g total fat (4g saturated fat); 362 cal; 15.1g carbohydrate; 45.4g protein; 7.8g fiber

A QUESADILLA (FROM QUESO, THE SPANISH WORD FOR CHEESE) IS A TORTILLA "SANDWICH" CONTAINING CHEESE AND ANY OF A WIDE NUMBER OF SPICY FILLING INGREDIENTS, WHICH IS GRILLED, FRIED OR TOASTED AND USUALLY SERVED WITH SALSA. WE COOKED THESE QUESADILLAS IN A FRYING PAN BUT YOU CAN COOK QUESADILLAS, ONE AT A TIME, IN A HEATED SANDWICH PRESS, IF YOU HAVE ONE.

corn and goat's cheese
QUESADILLAS

PREP + COOK TIME 30 MINUTES ✦ SERVES 4

2 corn cobs, trimmed
7½ ounces soft goat's cheese
8 8-inch flour tortillas
½ cup drained char-grilled red bell pepper, sliced thinly
2 tablespoons pickled sliced jalapeño chilies, drained
⅓ cup coarsely chopped fresh cilantro
¾ ounce butter
1½ ounces baby spinach leaves
1 lime, cut into wedges

1 Cook corn on heated oiled grill plate (or grill or barbecue) until browned lightly and tender; when cool enough to handle, cut kernels from cobs.
2 Spread cheese over tortillas. Top 4 of the tortillas with corn, bell peppers, chili and cilantro, season; top with remaining tortillas. Press around edges firmly to seal quesadillas.
3 Melt butter in medium frying pan; cook quesadillas, one at a time, until browned both sides and heated through.
4 Serve quesadillas with spinach and lime wedges.

nutritional count per serving 21.7g total fat (10g saturated fat); 519 cal; 57g carbohydrate; 19.8g protein; 8.6g fiber

lamb shanks in
CHILI SAUCE

PREP + COOK TIME 2 HOURS 30 MINUTES ☀ SERVES 4

3 ancho chilies
1 cup boiling water
1 tablespoon olive oil
8 french-trimmed lamb shanks
1 medium yellow onion, chopped finely
3 cloves garlic, crushed
1 teaspoon ground cumin
½ teaspoon ground cilantro
2 sprigs fresh thyme
4 cups beef stock
2 cups water, extra
2 dried bay leaves
⅓ cup loosely packed fresh cilantro leaves
2 limes, cut into wedges

1 Cover chilies with the boiling water in small heatproof bowl; stand 20 minutes. Discard stems and seeds from chilies; blend or process chilies with soaking liquid until smooth.

2 Heat oil in large saucepan; cook lamb, in batches, until browned. Remove from pan; drain on paper towel.

3 Drain fat from pan, add onion and garlic to same pan; cook, stirring, until onion softens. Add spices and chili mixture; cook, stirring, until fragrant.

4 Return lamb to pan with thyme, stock, the extra water and bay leaves; bring to the boil. Reduce heat; simmer, covered, about 1½ hours, skimming fat from surface occasionally, or until lamb is tender and almost falling off the bone. Uncover; simmer about 20 minutes or until sauce thickens slightly. Discard thyme and bay leaves; season to taste.

5 Divide lamb between serving bowls; top with cilantro. Serve with lime wedges and crusty bread.

nutritional count per serving 9.7g total fat (3.2g saturated fat); 373 cal; 4.9g carbohydrate; 65.3g protein; 1.1g fiber

spiced grilled beef
WITH CHILI BEANS

PREP + COOK TIME 1 HOUR 45 MINUTES (+ STANDING) ⚙ **SERVES 4**

PASILLA (PRONOUNCED PAH-SEE-YAH) CHILIES ARE THE WRINKLED, DRIED VERSION OF FRESH CHILACA CHILIES. ABOUT 8 INCHES IN LENGTH, A PASILLA IS ONLY MILDLY HOT, BUT POSSESSES A RICH FLAVOR THAT ADDS SMOKY DEPTH TO THE OVERALL RECIPE.

2   cups dried black beans
2   pasilla chilies
¼   cup boiling water
2   tablespoons olive oil
1   medium yellow onion, chopped finely
3   cloves garlic, crushed
¼   cup tomato paste
4   medium tomatoes, chopped coarsely
½   cup water
2   tablespoons lime juice
2   tablespoons light brown sugar
1   tablespoon dried marjoram
2   teaspoons smoked paprika
2   pounds beef rump steak
8   8-inch flour tortillas
1   small iceberg lettuce, trimmed, shredded finely
1   small red onion, sliced thinly
⅓   cup firmly packed fresh cilantro leaves
⅔   cup sour cream

1 Place beans in medium bowl, cover with water; stand overnight, drain.

2 Cook beans in large saucepan of boiling water, uncovered, until tender; drain. Rinse under cold water; drain.

3 Meanwhile, cover chilies with the boiling water in small heatproof bowl; stand 20 minutes. Discard stalks from chilies. Blend or process chilies with soaking liquid until smooth.

4 Heat half the oil in large saucepan; cook brown onion and garlic, stirring, until onion softens. Add chili mixture, paste, tomato, the water, juice and sugar; bring to the boil. Remove from heat; blend or process mixture until smooth.

5 Return chili mixture to pan; add beans, simmer, covered, 20 minutes. Uncover; simmer about 10 minutes or until sauce thickens. Season to taste.

6 Meanwhile, combine marjoram, paprika and remaining oil in large bowl; add beef, turn to coat in mixture, season. Cook beef on heated oiled grill plate (or grill or barbecue) until browned both sides and cooked as desired. Cover beef; stand 10 minutes then slice thinly.

7 Meanwhile, heat tortillas according to instructions on packet.

8 Serve tortillas topped with chili beans, red onion, lettuce, beef, cilantro and sour cream.

nutritional count per serving 49.8g total fat (20.4g saturated fat); 1234 cal; 96.2g carbohydrate; 92g protein; 21.4g fiber

chili lamb roasts with
BLACK BEAN SALAD

PREP + COOK TIME 1 HOUR 20 MINUTES (+ STANDING & REFRIGERATION) ✸ **SERVES 4**

1 cup dried black beans
2 mini lamb roasts
¼ cup olive oil
1 large yellow onion, chopped finely
1 clove garlic, crushed
1 fresh long green chili, chopped finely
1 teaspoon ground cumin
2 tablespoons red wine vinegar
1 large tomato, seeded, chopped coarsely
½ cup firmly packed fresh cilantro leaves
3 scallions, sliced thinly
2 tablespoons lime juice

CHILI MARINADE

3 fresh long green chilies, chopped finely
3 scallions, chopped finely
2 cloves garlic, crushed
1 teaspoon each ground allspice and dried thyme
1 teaspoon granulated sugar
1 tablespoon worcestershire sauce
1 tablespoon lime juice

1 Place beans in medium bowl, cover with water; stand overnight.
2 Combine ingredients for chili marinade in large bowl; add lamb, rub all over with marinade. Cover; refrigerate overnight.
3 Preheat oven to 350°F.
4 Drain beans; rinse under cold water. Cook beans in medium saucepan of boiling water, uncovered, about 20 minutes or until tender; drain.
5 Meanwhile, heat half the oil in medium flameproof casserole dish; cook lamb, uncovered, until browned all over. Roast lamb, uncovered, in oven, about 20 minutes or until cooked as desired. Cover lamb; stand 10 minutes then slice thickly.
6 Meanwhile, heat remaining oil in same cleaned saucepan; cook brown onion, garlic, chili and cumin, stirring, until onion softens. Add vinegar; cook, stirring, until liquid evaporates. Remove from heat.
7 Combine onion mixture, beans, tomato, cilantro, scallions and juice in large bowl; season to taste.
8 Serve lamb with salad.

nutritional count per serving 30.2g total fat (9g saturated fat); 563 cal; 22.4g carbohydrate; 49.8g protein; 12.8g fiber

BLACK BEANS, ALSO KNOWN AS TURTLE BEANS, ARE A COMMON INGREDIENT IN CARIBBEAN AND LATIN AMERICAN SOUPS, SALSAS AND SALADS. THEY ARE NOT THE SAME AS CHINESE BLACK BEANS, WHICH ARE FERMENTED SOY BEANS. THEY ARE AVAILABLE FROM GREENGROCERS AND DELICATESSENS.

LAMB FAJITAS

1¼ pounds lamb strips
3 cloves garlic, crushed
¼ cup lemon juice
2 teaspoons ground cumin
1 tablespoon olive oil
1 large red bell pepper, sliced thickly
1 large green bell pepper, sliced thickly
1 medium yellow bell pepper, sliced thickly
1 large red onion, sliced thickly
8 8-inch flour tortillas

GUACAMOLE

1 large avocado, chopped coarsely
¼ cup finely chopped fresh cilantro
1 tablespoon lime juice
1 small white onion, chopped finely

SALSA CRUDA

2 medium tomatoes, seeded, chopped finely
1 fresh long green chili, chopped finely
½ cup coarsely chopped fresh cilantro
1 clove garlic, crushed
1 small white onion, chopped finely
2 tablespoons lime juice

1 Combine lamb, garlic, juice, cumin and oil in large bowl. Cover; refrigerate.
2 Make guacamole.
3 Make salsa cruda.
4 Cook lamb, in batches, in heated oiled frying pan, stirring, until browned all over and cooked as desired. Remove from pan. Cover to keep warm.
5 Cook bell peppers and onion, in batches, in same pan, stirring, until just softened. Remove from pan.
6 Meanwhile, heat tortillas according to instructions on packet.
7 Return lamb and bell peppers mixture to pan; stir gently over medium heat until hot.
8 Divide lamb mixture between serving plates; serve with tortillas, guacamole and salsa cruda.

GUACAMOLE Gently combine ingredients in small bowl; season to taste.

SALSA CRUDA Combine ingredients in small bowl; season to taste.

nutritional count per serving 37.5g total fat (10.4g saturated fat); 772 cal; 62.3g carbohydrate; 45.8g protein; 8.4g fiber

seasoned roast pork with prune sauce
(recipe page 72)

seasoned roast pork
WITH PRUNE SAUCE

PREP + COOK TIME 2 HOURS (+ STANDING) ⚙ **SERVES 8**

(photograph page 71)

4-pound boneless loin of pork, rind on

SEASONING

- 1 tablespoon olive oil
- 1 medium yellow onion, chopped finely
- 2 cloves garlic, crushed
- 2 medium tomatoes, seeded, chopped finely
- ½ cup raisins
- ½ cup blanched almonds, chopped finely
- 9½ ounces ground pork and veal
- 1 cup dry breadcrumbs

PRUNE SAUCE

- 1 medium yellow onion, quartered
- 1 medium tomato, quartered
- 3 cloves garlic, unpeeled
- 2 tablespoons olive oil
- 2 chipotle chilies
- ⅓ cup blanched almonds
- ¾ cup seeded prunes
- 4 cloves
- 1 teaspoon ground cinnamon
- 2 tablespoons cider vinegar
- 1 cup chicken stock

1 Make seasoning.

2 Preheat oven to 425°F.

3 Place pork, fat-side down, on board; slice through thickest part of the pork horizontally, without cutting through the other side. Open pork out to form one large piece. Press seasoning mixture along one long side of pork; roll pork to enclose seasoning. Tie with kitchen string at ¾-inch intervals; place pork on wire rack in large shallow baking dish. Roast pork, uncovered, 30 minutes.

4 Reduce oven to 400°F. Roast pork, covered, about 1 hour or until cooked through.

5 Meanwhile, make prune sauce.

6 Remove pork from dish; cover pork loosely with foil, stand 15 minutes then slice thinly.

7 Serve pork with prune sauce.

SEASONING Heat oil in large frying pan; cook onion and garlic, stirring, until onion softens. Add tomato, raisins and nuts; simmer, uncovered, about 5 minutes or until thick. Cool. Combine tomato mixture, minced pork and veal, and breadcrumbs in medium bowl, season; mix well.

PRUNE SAUCE Preheat oven to 400°F. Place onion, tomato and garlic on oiled oven tray; drizzle with half the oil. Roast, uncovered, about 25 minutes or until vegetables soften. When cool enough to handle, peel tomato and garlic. Meanwhile, remove stems, seeds and membranes from chilies; chop chilies coarsely. Cover chilies with boiling water in small heatproof bowl; stand 20 minutes. Drain. Heat remaining oil in large frying pan; cook nuts, prunes and spices, stirring, until nuts are browned lightly. Blend or process nut mixture and vinegar until mixture forms a thick paste. Add drained chilies, onion, tomato and garlic; process until smooth. Add chili mixture and stock to same heated pan; simmer, stirring occasionally, until sauce is heated through. Season to taste.

nutritional count per serving 33.4g total fat (7.5g saturated fat); 669 cal; 23.6g carbohydrate; 66.9g protein; 4.9g fiber.

barbecued corn with
CHUNKY SALSA AND RICE

PREP + COOK TIME 50 MINUTES (+ REFRIGERATION) ⚙ **SERVES 4**

4   untrimmed ears of corn
2   teaspoons peanut oil
2   cloves garlic, crushed
1   small white onion, chopped finely
1   small red bell pepper, chopped finely
1   fresh long red chili, chopped finely
1½ cups white medium-grain rice
1   cup vegetable stock
1   cup water

CHUNKY SALSA

3   medium tomatoes, chopped coarsely
1   small white onion, chopped finely
¼   cup pickled sliced jalapeño chilies, drained
½   cup coarsely chopped fresh cilantro
1   clove garlic, crushed
2   tablespoons lime juice

1 Gently peel husk down ear of corn, keeping husk attached at base. Remove as much silk as possible then bring husk back over cob to re-wrap and enclose completely. Place corn in large bowl, add enough cold water to completely submerge corn.
2 Heat oil in medium saucepan; cook garlic, onion, bell peppers and chili, stirring, until onion softens. Add rice; cook, stirring, 1 minute. Add stock and the water; bring to the boil. Reduce heat; simmer, covered, about 20 minutes or until rice is just tender. Remove from heat; fluff rice with fork, season to taste.
3 Meanwhile, drain corn. Cook corn on heated oiled grill plate (or grill or barbecue) about 25 minutes or until corn is tender, turning occasionally.
4 Make chunky salsa.
5 Serve corn with rice and salsa.

CHUNKY SALSA Combine ingredients in medium bowl; season to taste.

nutritional count per serving 6.7g total fat (0.9g saturated fat); 608 cal; 114g carbohydrate; 20.6g protein; 16.9g fiber

3 eggs
¼ teaspoon salt
⅔ cup all-purpose flour
1½ cups milk
2 tablespoons olive oil
¾ cup coarsely grated cheddar cheese

MUSHROOM FILLING

¾ ounce butter
2 tablespoons olive oil
1 medium yellow onion, chopped finely
4 cloves garlic, crushed
1 fresh long red chili, chopped finely
1 pound button mushrooms, chopped finely
¼ cup finely chopped fresh cilantro

CILANTRO SAUCE

1 tablespoon olive oil
1 large yellow onion, chopped finely
4 cloves garlic, crushed
1 cup heavy cream
½ cup sour cream
¾ cup finely chopped fresh cilantro
½ cup coarsely grated cheddar cheese

mushroom crêpes with
CILANTRO SAUCE

PREP + COOK TIME 1 HOUR 30 MINUTES ⚙ SERVES 6

1 Whisk eggs, salt, flour, milk and oil in medium bowl until smooth. Cover; stand 30 minutes.

2 Meanwhile, make mushroom filling.

3 Heat oiled heavy-based crêpe pan or small frying pan; pour ¼ cup of batter into pan, tilting pan to coat base. Cook, over low heat, until browned lightly, loosening edge of crêpe with spatula. Turn crêpe; brown other side. Remove crêpe from pan; cover to keep warm. Repeat with remaining batter to make a total of 12 crêpes.

4 Preheat oven to 350°F.

5 Place heaped tablespoons of filling along center of each crêpe; roll crêpes to enclose filling. Place crêpes, in single layer, in oiled shallow baking dish; top with cheese.

6 Bake crêpes about 15 minutes or until filling is hot and cheese is browned lightly.

7 Meanwhile, make cilantro sauce.

8 Serve crêpes with sauce.

MUSHROOM FILLING   Heat butter and oil in large frying pan; cook onion, garlic and chili, stirring, until onion softens. Add mushrooms; cook, stirring, about 15 minutes or until mushrooms are soft and water has evaporated. Cool slightly; stir in cilantro, season to taste.

CILANTRO SAUCE   Heat oil in large frying pan; cook onion and garlic, stirring, until onion softens. Add cream; simmer, uncovered, about 10 minutes or until thickened. Remove from heat; stir in sour cream, cilantro and cheese. Season to taste.

nutritional count per serving   58g total fat (28.9g saturated fat); 686 cal; 19.1g carbohydrate; 19.1g protein; 4.4g fiber

black bean, corn and
CHIPOTLE STEW

PREP + COOK TIME 1 HOUR 15 MINUTES (+ STANDING) ✷ SERVES 4

1½ cups dried black beans
2 chipotle chilies
½ cup boiling water
1 tablespoon cumin seeds
2 ears of corn, trimmed
2 teaspoons olive oil
1 large yellow onion, chopped finely
1½ pounds canned crushed tomatoes
8 6-inch white corn tortillas

SALSA FRESCA
1 small red onion, chopped coarsely
1 small tomato, chopped coarsely
½ cup coarsely chopped fresh cilantro
1 lebanese cucumber, chopped coarsely
1 tablespoon olive oil
2 tablespoons lemon juice

1 Place beans in medium bowl, cover with water; stand overnight, drain. Rinse under cold water; drain. Cook beans in medium saucepan of boiling water about 15 minutes or until beans are just tender. Drain.
2 Preheat oven to 400°F.

3 Cover chilies with the boiling water in small heatproof bowl; stand 20 minutes. Discard stems; blend or process chili and soaking liquid until smooth.
4 Meanwhile, dry-fry cumin seeds in small frying pan, stirring, until fragrant.
5 Cook corn on heated oiled grill plate (or grill or barbecue) until browned lightly and just tender. When cool enough to handle, cut kernels from ears.
6 Heat oil in large flameproof dish; cook onion, stirring, until softened. Add drained beans, chili mixture, cumin, undrained tomatoes and half the corn; bring to the boil. Cook, uncovered, in oven, about 20 minutes or until sauce thickens. Season to taste.
7 Meanwhile, heat tortillas according to instructions on packet. Make salsa fresca.
8 Serve stew with tortillas and salsa.

SALSA FRESCA Combine remaining corn with salsa ingredients in medium bowl; season to taste.

nutritional count per serving 10.4g total fat (1.3g saturated fat); 440 cal; 61.3g carbohydrate; 26.2g protein; 19.5g fiber

TO ADD EXTRA HEAT SERVE SOME PICKLED SLICED JALAPENO CHILIES WITH THE TACOS.

- 1 tablespoon olive oil
- 1 medium yellow onion, chopped finely
- 1 pound ground chicken
- 1 ounce packet taco seasoning mix
- 12 ounces bottled thick and chunky taco sauce
- ½ cup water
- 10 stand 'n' stuff taco shells
- 1 cup finely shredded iceberg lettuce
- 1 medium carrot, grated coarsely
- 4 ounces cherry tomatoes, quartered
- ½ cup coarsely grated cheddar cheese
- ½ cup loosely packed fresh cilantro leaves
- ⅓ cup sour cream

1 Heat oil in large frying pan; cook onion, stirring, until softened. Add chicken; cook, stirring, until browned. Add taco seasoning; cook, stirring, until fragrant. Add half the taco sauce and the water; cook, stirring occasionally, about 7 minutes or until mixture thickens. Remove from heat; season to taste.
2 Meanwhile, heat taco shells according to directions on packet.
3 Divide chicken mixture into shells; top with lettuce, carrot, tomato, cheese, cilantro, sour cream and remaining sauce.

nutritional count per taco 35.9g total fat (13.3g saturated fat); 585 cal; 29.7g carbohydrate; 33.2g protein; 6.7g fiber

spicy

CHICKEN TACOS

PREP + COOK TIME 25 MINUTES ✷ MAKES 10

- ¼ cup light olive oil
- 2 medium green bell peppers, chopped coarsely
- 1 medium yellow onion, chopped coarsely
- 2 fresh small red thai (serrano) chilies, chopped finely
- 2 cloves garlic, crushed
- ¼ teaspoon ground white pepper
- 1 teaspoon ground cinnamon
- 4 medium tomatoes, chopped coarsely
- ¾ cup pimiento-stuffed green olives, chopped coarsely
- 2 tablespoons drained capers, rinsed, chopped coarsely
- 1 tablespoon lemon juice
- 2 1½-pound whole snapper

1 Heat oil in large frying pan; cook bell peppers, onion, chili and garlic, stirring, until onion softens. Add pepper, cinnamon and tomato; simmer, uncovered, stirring occasionally, about 10 minutes or until tomatoes have broken down and sauce is thick. Stir in olives, capers and juice; season to taste. Cool.
2 Preheat oven to 350°F.
3 Score fish three times each side through thickest part of flesh; place fish in large baking dish, season. Pour tomato mixture over fish.
4 Bake fish, uncovered, about 30 minutes or until fish is cooked through. Serve with lemon wedges.

nutritional count per serving 19.7g total fat (3.5g saturated fat); 409 cal; 8.1g carbohydrate; 46.7g protein; 5.5g fiber

snapper
VERACRUZ

PREP + COOK TIME 1 HOUR (+ COOLING) ✺ **SERVES 4**

paprika and parmesan polenta
WITH WALNUT AND BELL PEPPER SALSA

PREP + COOK TIME 1 HOUR (+ REFRIGERATION) ✸ **SERVES 6**

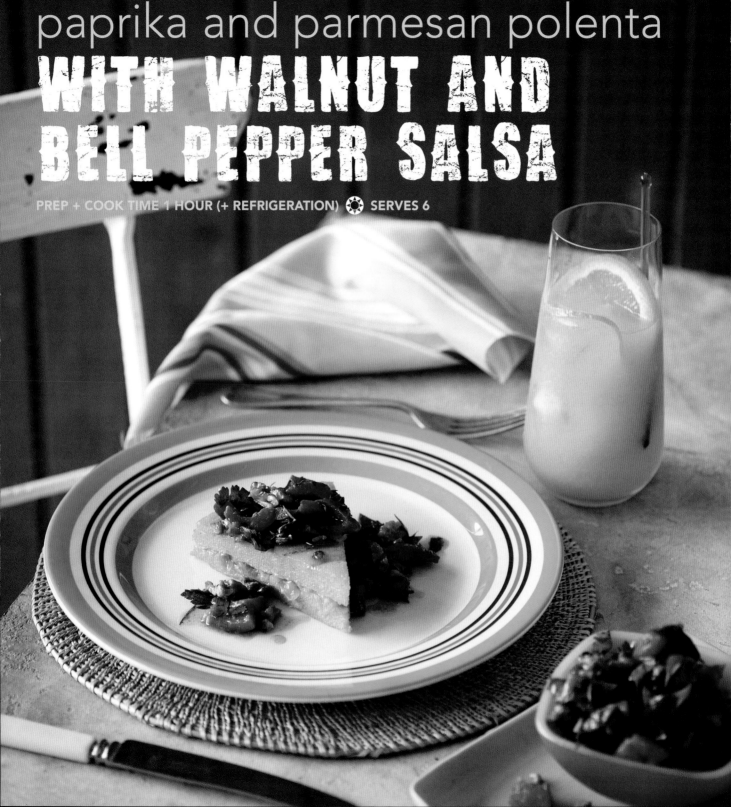

YOU CAN USE OLIVE OIL INSTEAD OF
THE WALNUT OIL, IF YOU PREFER.

¾ ounce butter

2 medium yellow onions, sliced thinly

1 tablespoon light brown sugar

4 cups water

1⅓ cups polenta

2 teaspoons smoked paprika

1 tablespoon red wine vinegar

1 cup coarsely grated parmesan cheese

WALNUT AND BELL PEPPER SALSA

2 large red bell peppers

1½ cups roasted walnuts, chopped coarsely

1 tablespoon red wine vinegar

¼ cup walnut oil

1 clove garlic, crushed

½ cup coarsely chopped fresh flat-leaf parsley

⅓ cup coarsely chopped fresh cilantro

1 Melt butter in medium frying pan; cook onion, stirring, until softened. Add sugar and 2 tablespoons of the water; cook, stirring, about 5 minutes or until onion caramelises. Cover to keep warm.

2 Oil deep 9-inch round cake pan. Bring remaining water to the boil in medium saucepan. Gradually add polenta and paprika, stirring constantly. Simmer, stirring, about 8 minutes or until polenta thickens. Stir in vinegar and cheese then spread half the polenta into pan. Spread onion mixture over polenta, spread remaining polenta over onion. Cover; refrigerate 3 hours or until firm.

3 Meanwhile, make walnut and bell pepper salsa.

4 Turn polenta onto board; cut into six wedges. Cook polenta, both sides, on heated oiled grill plate (or grill or barbecue) until browned lightly and hot. Serve polenta with salsa.

WALNUT AND BELL PEPPER SALSA Preheat grill (broiler). Quarter bell peppers, discard seeds and membranes. Place bell peppers, skin-side up, on oven tray; grill until skin blisters and blackens. Cover bell peppers pieces in plastic or paper for 5 minutes; peel away skin, chop coarsely. Combine bell peppers and remaining ingredients in small bowl; season to taste.

nutritional count per serving 51.8g total fat (10.6g saturated fat); 768 cal; 51.9g carbohydrate; 21.2g protein; 7.1g fiber

chicken quesadillas
WITH GUACAMOLE

PREP + COOK TIME 45 MINUTES ✸ SERVES 4

1 tablespoon olive oil

1 small red onion, chopped finely

2 cloves garlic, crushed

¼ teaspoon cayenne pepper

2 teaspoons ground cumin

1 medium red bell pepper, chopped finely

1 medium green bell pepper, chopped finely

3 cups shredded barbecued chicken

8 8-inch flour tortillas

2 cups coarsely grated cheddar cheese

⅓ cup loosely packed fresh cilantro leaves

GUACAMOLE

2 large avocados, chopped coarsely

½ small red onion, chopped finely

1 large tomato, seeded, chopped finely

2 tablespoons lime juice

1 tablespoon finely chopped fresh cilantro

1 Heat oil in large frying pan; cook onion and garlic, stirring, until onion softens. Add spices and bell peppers; cook, stirring, until bell peppers soften. Remove from heat; stir in chicken. Season to taste.

2 Place one tortilla on board; top with ¼ cup of the cheese, then a quarter of the chicken mixture and another ¼ cup of the cheese. Top with a second tortilla. Repeat with remaining tortillas, cheese and chicken mixture.

3 Cook quesadillas, one at a time, in same oiled pan, over medium heat, until golden brown both sides. Remove from pan; cover to keep warm while cooking remaining quesadillas.

4 Meanwhile, make guacamole.

5 Serve quesadillas, cut into quarters, with guacamole, cilantro and, if you like, a dollop of sour cream.

GUACAMOLE Mash avocado in medium bowl; stir in remaining ingredients. Season to taste.

nutritional count per serving 66g total fat (22.7g saturated fat); 1051 cal; 54.3g carbohydrate; 57.1g protein; 6.7g fiber

pork ribs with chorizo and
SMOKED PAPRIKA

PREP + COOK TIME 2 HOURS 15 MINUTES SERVES 4

3 pounds american-style pork spareribs
4 cloves garlic, crushed
2 teaspoons smoked paprika
1 tablespoon olive oil
1 cured chorizo sausage, sliced thinly
1 tablespoon olive oil, extra
1 medium red onion, chopped coarsely
1 medium red bell pepper, chopped coarsely
1 tablespoon light brown sugar
1½ pounds canned chopped tomatoes
1 cup chicken stock

1 Cut between bones of pork to separate into individual ribs. Combine garlic, paprika and oil in small bowl; rub over pork ribs.

2 Preheat oven to 325°F.

3 Cook chorizo in heated large flameproof baking dish, stirring, until browned lightly. Remove from dish with slotted spoon; drain on paper towel.

4 Cook ribs, in same dish, in batches, until browned. Drain on paper towel.

5 Add extra oil, onion and bell pepper to same dish; cook, stirring, until onion softens. Return ribs and chorizo to dish with sugar, undrained tomatoes and stock; bring to the boil.

6 Cover dish tightly with foil; cook, in oven, 1 hour. Remove foil; cook further 30 minutes or until ribs are tender. Season to taste.

nutritional count per serving 38.5g total fat (11.4g saturated fat); 602 cal; 15.6g carbohydrate; 49.2g protein; 4.1g fiber

BEANS AND RICE

THE STEM OF ZUCCHINI IS THE BABY ZUCCHINI ATTACHED TO THE FLOWER. YOU NEED TO COOK ABOUT 1½ CUPS WHITE LONG-GRAIN RICE FOR THIS RECIPE. SPREAD COOKED RICE ON A FLAT TRAY AND REFRIGERATE, UNCOVERED, OVERNIGHT BEFORE USING.

saffron rice
WITH ZUCCHINI FLOWERS

PREP + COOK TIME 30 MINUTES ⊛ SERVES 4

12 zucchini flowers, stem attached
1½ ounces butter
1 large red onion, cut into wedges
2 teaspoons caraway seeds
1 clove garlic, crushed
4 cups cooked white long-grain rice
1 teaspoon ground turmeric
pinch saffron threads
¼ cup flaked almonds, roasted

1 Remove flowers from zucchini; discard stamens from flowers. Slice zucchini thinly.
2 Melt butter in large frying pan; cook onion, seeds and garlic, stirring, until onion softens. Add sliced zucchini; cook, stirring, until tender. Add rice, spices and zucchini flowers; cook, stirring, until hot. Stir in half the nuts; season to taste.
3 Serve sprinkled with remaining nuts.

nutritional count per serving 12.9g total fat (6.2g saturated fat); 418 cal; 65.3g carbohydrate; 8g protein; 3.6g fiber

1 medium yellow onion, quartered
2 large tomatoes, quartered
2 cloves garlic, unpeeled
2 tablespoons olive oil
½ teaspoon chili powder
1½ cups white long-grain rice
2 cups chicken stock
1 small carrot, sliced thinly
½ cup frozen peas
4 ounces canned corn, drained
⅓ cup coarsely chopped fresh cilantro

1 Preheat oven to 400°F.
2 Place onion, tomato and garlic on oiled oven tray; drizzle with half the oil. Roast, uncovered, about 25 minutes or until vegetables soften. When cool enough to handle, peel tomato and garlic.
3 Blend or process onion, tomato, garlic and chili powder until smooth; you need 2 cups puree.
4 Heat remaining oil in medium saucepan; cook rice, stirring, 3 minutes. Add tomato mixture; cook, stirring, about 8 minutes or until almost all of the liquid is evaporated. Add stock, carrot, peas and corn; bring to the boil. Reduce heat; simmer, covered, over low heat, about 10 minutes or until rice is tender and liquid is absorbed. Remove from heat; stand, covered, 10 minutes. Fluff rice with a fork; season to taste. Serve sprinkled with cilantro.

nutritional count per serving 7.9g total fat (1.2g saturated fat); 416 cal; 72.9g carbohydrate; 10g protein; 5.3g fiber

MEXICAN RICE

PREP + COOK TIME 1 HOUR ✺ SERVES 4

1¾ cups dried kidney beans
6 cups water
1 small yellow onion, chopped coarsely
1 clove garlic, crushed
1 dried bay leaf
½ fresh small green chili, chopped finely
2 tablespoons olive oil
1 small brown onion, chopped finely
1 large tomato, peeled, chopped finely

1 Combine beans, the water, coarsely chopped onion, garlic, bay leaf and chili in large saucepan; bring to the boil. Reduce heat; simmer, covered, about 1½ hours or until beans are tender.
2 Drain bean mixture, discard bay leaf; reserve ½ cup cooking liquid. Blend or process bean mixture with reserved cooking liquid until coarsely mashed.
3 Heat oil in large frying pan; cook finely chopped onion, stirring, until onion softens. Add tomato; cook, stirring, until tomato softens. Stir in bean mixture; cook, stirring, about 10 minutes or until thickened. Season to taste.

nutritional count per serving
7.2g total fat (1g saturated fat); 240 cal;
23g carbohydrate; 13.9g protein;
13.4g fiber

SERVING SUGGESTION
Serve as a dip with corn chips or use as a vegetarian filling for tacos, quesadillas or burritos.

REFRIED BEANS

PREP + COOK TIME 2 HOURS 30 MINUTES ✺ SERVES 6

red beans
AND RICE

PREP + COOK TIME 1 HOUR ✸ **SERVES 4**

RED BEANS AND RICE IS A FILLING AND BUDGET-
FRIENDLY DISH. IF YOU LIKE, SERVE WITH GRILLED
CHICKEN FOR A MEATIER MEAL OR IT CAN BE
SERVED AS A SIDE DISH TO ACCOMPANY MANY
OF THE MAIN MEALS IN THIS BOOK. YOU NEED
ONE TRIMMED EAR OF CORN TO GET THE AMOUNT
OF CORN KERNELS REQUIRED FOR THIS RECIPE;
YOU CAN USE THE SAME AMOUNT OF DRAINED
CANNED CORN OR FROZEN CORN, IF YOU PREFER.

2   rindless bacon slices, chopped coarsely
1   medium yellow onion, chopped finely
1   small red bell pepper, chopped finely
2   cloves garlic, crushed
1   tablespoon tomato paste
1   tablespoon red wine vinegar
1   teaspoon smoked paprika
2   cups white long-grain rice
1   dried bay leaf
1   cup chicken stock
2¼ cups water
13 ounces canned kidney beans, drained, rinsed
½   cup corn kernels
1   tablespoon lime juice

1 Cook bacon in heated large frying pan, stirring,
until starting to crisp. Add onion, bell pepper and
garlic; cook, stirring until onion softens.
2 Add paste, vinegar and paprika; cook, stirring,
1 minute. Add rice; cook, stirring, 2 minutes.
3 Add bay leaf, stock, the water and beans;
bring to the boil. Reduce heat; simmer, covered,
20 minutes. Add corn; cook, covered, about
5 minutes or until rice is tender. Remove from
heat; stand, covered, 5 minutes. Stir in juice;
season to taste.

nutritional count per serving   3.3g total fat
(1g saturated fat); 530 cal; 99.3g carbohydrate;
20.8g protein; 7.1g fiber

1 large green bell pepper
2 medium yellow onions, quartered
4 cloves garlic, unpeeled
2 fresh small green chilies
¼ cup olive oil
3 cups chicken stock
⅓ cup each firmly packed fresh flat-leaf parsley leaves and cilantro leaves
1½ cups white long-grain rice

1 Preheat oven to 400°F.
2 Quarter bell pepper; discard seeds and membranes. Place bell pepper, onion, garlic and chili on oiled oven tray; drizzle with 1 tablespoon oil. Roast, uncovered, about 25 minutes or until vegetables soften. When cool enough to handle, peel bell pepper and garlic; discard stems from chilis.
3 Blend or process bell pepper, onion, garlic and chili with 1 cup stock until combined. Add herbs; blend or process until smooth.
4 Heat remaining oil in medium saucepan; cook rice, stirring, about 3 minutes or until rice is browned lightly. Stir in herb mixture and remaining stock; bring to the boil. Reduce heat; simmer, covered, about 15 minutes or until rice is tender and liquid is absorbed. Remove from heat; stand, covered, 10 minutes. Fluff rice with a fork; season to taste.

nutritional count per serving 14.4g total fat (2.2g saturated fat); 440 cal; 67.3g carbohydrate; 9g protein; 2.7g fiber

GREEN RICE

PREP + COOK TIME 50 MINUTES 🔅 SERVES 4

DRUNKEN BEANS

PREP + COOK TIME 1 HOUR 50 MINUTES (+ STANDING) ⚙ SERVES 4

1 cup dried pinto beans
3 rindless bacon slices, chopped coarsely
1 medium yellow onion, chopped finely
1 clove garlic, crushed
1 teaspoon ground cumin
½ teaspoon cayenne pepper
1 tablespoon tomato paste
12½ ounces canned crushed tomatoes
1 cup water
1 cup beer
1 tablespoon worcestershire sauce
2 tablespoons light brown sugar

1 Place beans in medium bowl, cover with water; stand overnight. Drain.
2 Cook bacon, onion, garlic and spices in oiled large saucepan, stirring, until onion softens.
3 Add drained beans and remaining ingredients to pan; bring to the boil. Reduce heat; simmer, covered, about 1½ hours or until beans are just tender. Season to taste.

nutritional count per serving 4.8g total fat (1.5g saturated fat); 303 cal; 32.1g carbohydrate; 21.6g protein; 12.8g fiber

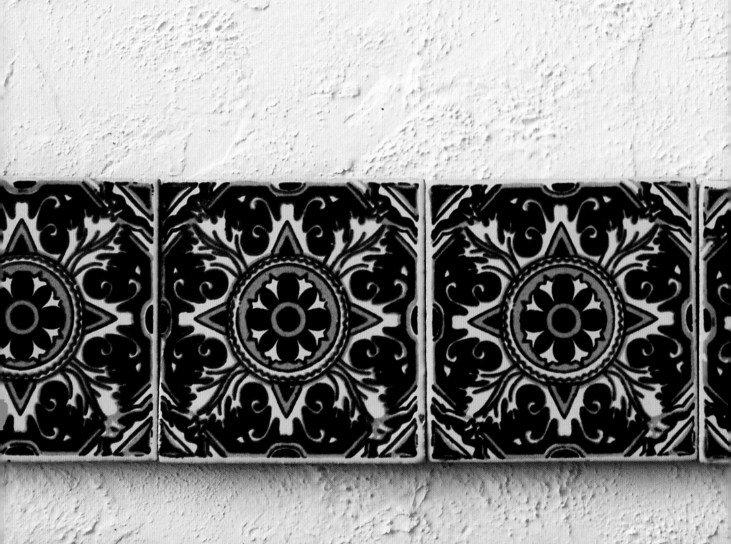

SALSAS
AND SAUCES

HOT SAUCE IS THE PERFECT CONDIMENT TO USE IF YOU WANT TO ADD EXTRA SPICE TO YOUR MEAL. SPOON A LITTLE HOT SAUCE ON ENCHILADAS, TACOS OR EVEN SCRAMBLED EGGS, IF YOU LIKE.

- 3 ancho chilies
- 1 cup boiling water
- 6 medium ripe tomatoes, chopped coarsely
- 4 cloves garlic, quartered
- 1 small yellow onion, chopped coarsely
- 3 cloves
- 2 tablespoons red wine vinegar
- 1 teaspoon dried thyme leaves
- ½ teaspoon dried oregano leaves
- ½ teaspoon ground cumin
- 2 tablespoons olive oil

1 Cover chilies with the boiling water in small heatproof bowl; stand 20 minutes.
2 Meanwhile, blend or process tomato until smooth.
3 Discard stalks from chilies; blend or process chili and soaking liquid with garlic, onion, cloves, vinegar, herbs and cumin until smooth.
4 Heat oil in large frying pan; cook chili mixture, stirring, until mixture comes to the boil. Add tomato mixture; simmer, uncovered, stirring occasionally, about 1 hour or until reduced to about 3 cups. Season to taste; cool.

nutritional count per ¼ cup
3.1g total fat (0.4g saturated fat); 42 cal; 1.9g carbohydrate; 0.9g protein; 1.2g fiber

HOT SAUCE

PREP + COOK TIME 1 HOUR 30 MINUTES ✷ MAKES 3 CUPS

mango and
AVOCADO SALSA

PREP TIME 15 MINUTES  **MAKES 2½ CUPS**

1   medium mango, chopped coarsely
1   large avocado, chopped coarsely
1   small red onion, chopped finely
1   small red bell pepper, chopped finely
1   fresh small red thai (serrano) chili, chopped finely
2   tablespoons lime juice

1 Combine ingredients in medium bowl; season to taste.

nutritional count per tablespoon   1.7g total fat (0.4g saturated fat); 24 cal; 1.6g carbohydrate; 0.4g protein; 0.4g fiber

SERVING SUGGESTION
Serve with roasted corn, grilled chicken or salmon fillets.

grilled corn and
ZUCCHINI SALSA

PREP + COOK TIME 30 MINUTES ✸ **MAKES 7 CUPS**

2   trimmed ears of corn
3   ounces baby zucchini, halved lengthways
2   large avocados, chopped coarsely
6½   ounces grape tomatoes, halved
1   medium red onion, sliced thickly
¼   cup coarsely chopped fresh cilantro
1   tablespoon sweet chili sauce
⅓   cup lime juice
2   fresh small red thai (serrano) chilies, sliced thinly

1 Cook corn and zucchini on heated oiled grill plate (or grill or barbecue) until tender and browned lightly. When cool enough to handle, remove kernels from cobs.

2 Place corn and zucchini in large bowl with avocado, tomato, onion and cilantro. Add combined sauce, juice and chili; toss gently to combine. Season to taste.

nutritional count per tablespoon 1.3g total fat (0.3g saturated fat); 20 cal; 1.4g carbohydrate; 0.5g protein; 0.5g fiber

black bean and
MANGO SALSA

PREP + COOK TIME 1 HOUR 40 MINUTES (+ STANDING) ✦ SERVES 6

1 cup dried black beans
1 lebanese cucumber, seeded, sliced thinly
1 medium mango, chopped finely
1 cup loosely packed fresh cilantro leaves

SWEET CHILI DRESSING
1 tablespoon olive oil
1 tablespoon sweet chili sauce
1 tablespoon lime juice

1 Place beans in medium bowl, cover with water; stand overnight. Drain.
2 Cook beans in medium saucepan of boiling water until tender; drain.
3 Meanwhile, make sweet chili dressing.
4 Place beans in medium bowl with dressing and remaining ingredients; toss gently to combine, season to taste.

SWEET CHILI DRESSING Combine ingredients in small bowl.

nutritional count per serving
9.9g total fat (1.5g saturated fat); 189 cal; 9.7g carbohydrate; 11.6g protein; 7.8g fiber

2 medium avocados
½ small red onion, chopped finely
1 medium plum tomato, seeded, chopped finely
1 tablespoon lime juice
¼ cup coarsely chopped fresh cilantro

1 Mash avocados in medium bowl; stir in remaining ingredients. Season to taste.

nutritional count per tablespoon 2.6g total fat (0.6g saturated fat); 26 cal; 0.2g carbohydrate; 0.3g protein; 0.2g fiber

SERVING SUGGESTION

Serve as a dip with corn chips; it also goes well with nachos, burritos and fajitas.

GUACAMOLE

PREP TIME 10 MINUTES MAKES 2½ CUPS

SWEET TREATS

FLAN DE CAFE

PREP + COOK TIME 50 MINUTES (+ REFRIGERATION) ⚙ MAKES 6

¾ cup superfine sugar
¾ cup water
6 eggs
⅓ cup superfine sugar, extra
2 tablespoons coffee-flavored liqueur
1 tablespoon instant coffee granules
1 tablespoon water, extra
1½ cups milk
1¼ cups heavy cream

1 Preheat oven to 325°F.

2 Stir sugar and the water in medium saucepan over heat, without boiling, until sugar dissolves. Bring to the boil; boil, uncovered, without stirring, about 5 minutes or until mixture is golden brown. Pour evenly into six 1-cup ovenproof dishes.

3 Whisk eggs and extra sugar together in medium bowl; stir in liqueur and combined coffee and the extra water.

4 Bring milk and cream to the boil in medium saucepan. Remove from heat; allow bubbles to subside. Gradually whisk milk mixture into egg mixture; strain into jug.

5 Place dishes in baking dish; pour custard into dishes. Pour enough boiling water into baking dish to come halfway up sides of dishes.

6 Bake flans about 30 minutes or until just set. Remove dishes from water; cool to room temperature. Refrigerate overnight.

7 Turn flans onto serving plates, serve with extra whipped cream and orange rind, if you like.

nutritional count per flan 26.9g total fat (15.9g saturated fat); 326 cal; 48.1g carbohydrate; 10g protein; 0.1g fiber

IT IS FINE TO USE JUST ONE 10 FLUID OZ CARTON OF CREAM FOR THIS RECIPE.

grilled bananas with
COCONUT SYRUP

PREP + COOK TIME 15 MINUTES ✷ SERVES 4

⅓ cup water
¼ cup firmly packed light brown sugar
¼ cup coconut-flavored liqueur
4 large ripe bananas
2 teaspoons finely grated lime rind
¼ cup shredded coconut, toasted

1 Stir the water and sugar in small saucepan over heat, without boiling, until sugar dissolves; bring to the boil. Reduce heat; simmer, uncovered, without stirring, about 3 minutes or until syrup thickens slightly. Remove from heat; stir in liqueur.
2 Split bananas lengthways; brush about a quarter of the syrup mixture over the cut-sides of bananas.
3 Cook bananas, cut-side down, on heated lightly oiled grill plate (or grill or barbecue) until browned lightly and heated through.
4 Meanwhile, heat remaining syrup mixture in small saucepan until hot. Remove from heat; stir in rind.
5 Serve hot bananas drizzled with syrup; sprinkle with coconut.

nutritional count per serving
3.5g total fat (2.6g saturated fat);
267 cal; 47g carbohydrate;
2.6g protein; 3.7g fiber

WE USED MALIBU, A RUM-BASED COCONUT LIQUEUR, FOR THIS RECIPE.

SERVING SUGGESTION
Serve with whipped cream or ice-cream.

4 eggs
¼ cup superfine sugar
1¾ all-purpose flour
½ cup self-raising flour
½ teaspoon salt
vegetable oil, for shallow-frying
1¼ cups superfine sugar, extra
1½ teaspoons ground cinnamon

1 Beat eggs and sugar in small bowl with electric mixer until thick and creamy. Transfer mixture to large bowl; stir in sifted flours and salt, in two batches. Knead dough on floured surface until smooth and no longer sticky. Wrap in plastic; stand 20 minutes.
2 Divide dough into 16 portions. Roll each portion on floured surface into 4¾-inch rounds.
3 Heat oil in large frying pan; shallow-fry pastries, one at a time, turning once, until browned lightly. Drain on absorbent paper.
4 Toss hot pastries in combined extra sugar and cinnamon. Serve warm or cold.

nutritional count per pastry 5.9g total fat (1g saturated fat); 131 cal; 32.2g carbohydrate; 3.9g protein; 0.8g fiber

fried
SWEET PASTRIES

PREP + COOK TIME 45 MINUTES (+ STANDING) ⚙ MAKES 16

ROYAL EGGS

PREP + COOK TIME 50 MINUTES (+ STANDING) ⚙ SERVES 4

12 egg yolks
2 teaspoons baking powder
1 teaspoon water
1 teaspoon melted butter

CINNAMON SYRUP

2 cups superfine sugar
1 cup water
3 cinnamon sticks, broken
½ cup dry sherry
2 tablespoons lime juice
⅓ cup raisins
⅓ cup pine nuts, roasted

1 Preheat oven to 325°F. Grease deep 8-inch square cake pan; line base with baking paper, grease paper.
2 Beat egg yolks and baking powder in small bowl with electric mixer until thick and creamy; fold in the water and butter. Pour mixture into pan.
3 Place pan in baking dish; add enough boiling water to dish to come half way up sides of pan.
4 Bake cake about 15 minutes or until firm. Remove pan from water; stand 10 minutes.
5 Meanwhile, make cinnamon syrup.
6 Carefully turn cake onto board; cut into squares. Place squares in deep heatproof dish, pour over hot syrup; stand until syrup is cool.

CINNAMON SYRUP Stir sugar, the water, cinnamon, sherry and juice in medium saucepan, over heat, without boiling, until sugar dissolves; bring to the boil. Reduce heat; simmer, uncovered, without stirring, about 3 minutes or until thickened slightly. Remove from heat; stir in raisins and nuts.

nutritional count per serving 26.8g total fat (7g saturated fat); 356 cal; 120g carbohydrate; 11.4g protein; 1.3g fiber

coconut and pineapple
CHIMICHANGAS

PREP + COOK TIME 45 MINUTES ✳ MAKES 8

⅔ cup canned crushed pineapple, drained
½ cup finely chopped raisins
⅓ cup apricot jam
2 teaspoons ground cinnamon
½ cup shredded coconut
8 6-inch flour tortillas
vegetable oil, for deep-frying
1 tablespoon confectioners' sugar

1 Combine pineapple, raisins, jam, cinnamon and coconut in medium bowl.
2 Heat tortillas according to instructions on packet.
3 Divide pineapple mixture evenly between tortillas. Roll tortillas up firmly, folding in sides; secure with toothpicks.
4 Heat oil in wok or large frying pan; deep-fry tortilla rolls, in batches, until browned lightly. Drain on absorbent paper. Remove toothpicks.
5 Dust chimichangas with sifted icing sugar. Cut each chimichanga in half; serve with ice-cream or whipped cream, if you like.

nutritional count per chimichanga 8.2g total fat (3.3g saturated fat); 204 cal; 29.8g carbohydrate; 2.4g protein; 2.3g fiber

mexican
WEDDING COOKIES

PREP + COOK TIME 55 MINUTES (+ REFRIGERATION) **MAKES 34**

8 ounces butter, softened
¾ cup superfine sugar
2 cups all-purpose flour
½ cup finely chopped blanched almonds
½ cup finely chopped pecans
1 tablespoon finely grated orange rind
1 teaspoon vanilla extract
1 egg yolk
¼ cup confectioners' sugar

1 Preheat oven to 350°F. Line oven trays with baking paper.
2 Beat butter and sugar in small bowl with electric mixer until light and fluffy. Stir in sifted flour, nuts, rind, extract and egg yolk.
3 Shape level tablespoons of dough into rectangles; place biscuits, about 1-inch apart, on trays. Cover; refrigerate 30 minutes.
4 Bake biscuits about 25 minutes. Stand on trays 5 minutes, before transferring to wire racks to cool. Dust with sifted icing sugar.

nutritional count per cookie 8.8g total fat (4.2g saturated fat); 117 cal; 12.7g carbohydrate; 1.7g protein; 0.7g fiber

1 lime
1½ cups superfine sugar
1 cinnamon stick
6 cloves
2½ cups water
4 medium pink guavas
½ teaspoon vanilla extract

1 Using vegetable peeler, peel rind thinly from lime; cut rind into thin strips. Squeeze 1 tablespoon juice from lime.

2 Combine rind, juice, sugar, cinnamon, cloves and the water in medium saucepan; stir over heat, without boiling, until sugar dissolves. Simmer, covered, 20 minutes.

3 Peel guavas; cut into quarters, discard seeds.

4 Add guavas to syrup; simmer, covered loosely, about 10 minutes, or until guavas are tender. Cool guavas in syrup.

5 Remove guavas from syrup; place in medium heatproof bowl. Strain syrup through fine sieve; discard cinnamon and cloves.

6 Return syrup to same pan; simmer, uncovered, about 10 minutes or until reduced to about 1¼ cups. Remove pan from heat; stir in extract. Pour syrup over guavas; cool. Cover; refrigerate.

7 Serve guavas and syrup, if you like, with yogurt, whipped cream or ice-cream.

nutritional count per serving 0.5g total fat (0.1g saturated fat); 34 cal; 3.4g carbohydrate; 0.7g protein; 5.1g fiber

poached guavas
IN SPICY SYRUP

PREP + COOK TIME 1 HOUR (+ COOLING) ✸ **SERVES 4**

THREE KINGS BREAD

PREP + COOK TIME 1 HOUR (+ STANDING) SERVES 12

1 tablespoon dried yeast

1 teaspoon superfine sugar

¼ cup warm water

2½ cups all-purpose flour

1 teaspoon salt

3 ounces butter, chopped finely

¼ cup superfine sugar, extra

2 teaspoons each finely grated orange and lemon rind

2 eggs, beaten lightly

4 egg yolks

¼ cup coarsely chopped glacé figs

¼ cup coarsely chopped glacé apricots

¼ cup coarsely chopped raisins

¼ cup coarsely chopped roasted walnuts

1 egg, beaten lightly, extra

1 slice glacé orange, chopped coarsely

1 tablespoon coarsely chopped roasted walnuts, extra

ORANGE ICING

1¼ cups confectioners' sugar

2 tablespoons orange juice

1 Combine yeast, sugar and the water in small bowl. Cover; stand in warm place about 10 minutes or until mixture is frothy.

2 Sift flour and salt into large bowl; rub in butter. Stir in extra sugar and rind. Combine yeast mixture, eggs and egg yolks in medium bowl; stir into flour mixture, mix to a soft dough.

3 Knead dough on floured surface about 10 minutes or until smooth and elastic. Place dough in large oiled bowl. Cover; stand in warm place about 1 hour or until dough doubles in size.

4 Toss figs, apricots, raisins and nuts in about 1 tablespoon of plain flour, breaking up any chunks of fruit. Turn dough onto floured surface, add fruit and nut mixture; knead until smooth.

5 Roll dough into 19¼-inch log; shape log into ring, press ends together firmly. Place ring on greased oven tray around a greased 3¾-inch ovenproof dish so the ring stays in shape during cooking. Cover; stand in warm place about 50 minutes or until doubled in size.

6 Preheat oven to 400°F.

7 Brush ring with extra egg; bake 10 minutes. Reduce oven to 350°F. Bake bread about 15 minutes. Place bread on wire rack over tray, stand 30 minutes.

8 Make orange icing.

9 Pour icing over bread; decorate with glacé orange and sprinkle with extra nuts.

ORANGE ICING Combine sifted icing sugar and juice in small pitcher.

nutritional count per serving 12.5g total fat (5.7g saturated fat); 342 cal; 55.1g carbohydrate; 7.3g protein; 2.4g fiber

1 cup water
1 tablespoon superfine sugar
3 ounces butter, chopped coarsely
1 cup all-purpose flour
2 eggs
vegetable oil, for deep-frying

ANISEED SUGAR

5 star anise
½ cup superfine sugar

1 Make aniseed sugar.
2 Bring the water, sugar and butter to the boil in medium saucepan. Add sifted flour; beat with wooden spoon over high heat until mixture comes away from base and side of pan to form a smooth ball. Transfer mixture to small bowl; beat in eggs, one at a time, with electric mixer until mixture becomes glossy.
3 Spoon mixture into piping bag fitted with a ½-inch fluted tube.
4 Heat oil in large saucepan; pipe 2¼-inch lengths of batter into oil (cut off lengths with a knife). Deep-fry churros, in batches, about 6 minutes or until browned lightly and crisp. Drain on paper towel.
5 Roll churros in aniseed sugar. Serve warm.

ANISEED SUGAR Blend or process ingredients until ground finely.

nutritional count per churro 3.4g total fat (1.6g saturated fat); 59 cal; 6.8g carbohydrate; 0.9g protein; 0.2g fiber

CHURROS

PREP + COOK TIME 30 MINUTES **MAKES 35**

strawberry and peach
TEQUILA POPSICLES

3 medium peaches, chopped coarsely
¼ cup grated palm sugar
⅓ cup tequila
1 tablespoon cointreau
1 tablespoon lemon juice
1 pound strawberries, chopped coarsely

1 Blend or process peaches until smooth. Push peaches through a sieve into medium bowl; stir in half the sugar, half the tequila, cointreau and juice.
2 Divide half the peach mixture into 12 ⅓ cup paddle pop moulds (or paper cups); reserve remaining peach mixture. Freeze about 30 minutes or until surface is firm.
3 Meanwhile, blend or process strawberries until smooth. Push strawberries through a sieve into medium bowl; stir in remaining sugar and tequila.
4 Press paddle pop stick firmly into each popsicle. Divide half the strawberry mixture into moulds; reserve remaining strawberry mixture. Freeze about 30 minutes or until surface is firm.
5 Divide remaining peach mixture into moulds; freeze about 30 minutes or until surface is firm.
6 Divide remaining strawberry mixture into moulds; freeze popsicles overnight.

nutritional count per popsicle   0.1g total fat
(0g saturated fat); 77 cal; 12.5g carbohydrate;
1g protein; 1.4g fiber

GLOSSARY

ALLSPICE also called jamaican pepper or pimento; tastes like a combination of nutmeg, cumin, clove and cinnamon. Sold whole or ground.

ALMONDS
blanched brown skins removed.
flaked paper-thin slices.
slivered small pieces cut lengthways.

BAKING POWDER a raising agent consisting mainly of two parts cream of tartar to one part bicarbonate of soda. Also available gluten free.

BAY LEAVES aromatic leaves from the bay tree available fresh or dried; adds a strong, slightly peppery flavor.

BEANS
black also called turtle beans or black kidney beans; an earthy-flavored dried bean completely different from the better-known Chinese black beans (fermented soybeans). Used mostly in Mexican and South American cooking.
borlotti also called roman or pink beans, can be eaten fresh or dried. Interchangeable with pinto beans due to their similarity in appearance— pale pink or beige with dark red streaks.
kidney medium-sized red bean, slightly floury in texture yet sweet in flavour; sold dried or canned, it's often found in bean mixes.
mexican-style a canned mixture of either kidney or pinto beans cooked with tomato, peppers, onion, garlic and various spices.
pinto similar to borlotti, a plump, kidney-shaped, beige bean speckled with brown.
refried pinto beans, cooked twice— soaked and boiled, then mashed and fried, traditionally in lard. A Mexican staple, frijoles refritos or refried beans are available canned in supermarkets.

BELL PEPPER also called pepper. Discard seeds and membranes before use.

BLOOD ORANGE a virtually seedless citrus fruit with blood-red-streaked rind and flesh; sweet, non-acidic, salmon-colored pulp and juice with slight strawberry or raspberry overtones. The rind is not as bitter as an ordinary orange.

BREADCRUMBS
fresh bread, usually white, processed into crumbs.
packaged prepared fine-textured but crunchy white breadcrumbs; good for coating foods that are to be fried.
stale crumbs made by grating or processing one- or two-day-old bread.

BUTTER we use salted butter unless stated otherwise; 1 stick equals 4 ounces.

BUTTERMILK originally the term given to the slightly sour liquid left after butter was churned from cream, today it is made from no-fat or low-fat milk to which specific bacterial cultures have been added. Despite its name, it is actually low in fat.

CAPERS the grey-green buds of a warm climate (usually Mediterranean) shrub, sold either dried and salted or pickled in a vinegar brine. Capers should be rinsed before using.

CARAWAY SEEDS small dried seed from a member of the parsley family; has a sharp anise flavor.

CAYENNE PEPPER a thin-fleshed, long, extremely hot dried red chili, usually purchased ground.

CHEESE
cheddar semi-hard, yellow to off-white, sharp-tasting cheese.
cream commonly called philadelphia or philly; a soft cow's-milk cheese, its fat content ranges from 14 to 33%.
goat's made from goat's milk, has an earthy, strong taste. Available in soft, crumbly and firm textures, in various shapes and sizes, and sometimes rolled in ash or herbs.
parmesan also known as parmigiano, parmesan is a hard, grainy cow's-milk cheese that originated in the Parma region of Italy. The curd is salted in brine for a month before being aged up to two years in humid conditions.

CHICKEN
breast fillet breast halved, skinned and boned.
drumstick leg with skin and bone intact.
thigh cutlet thigh with skin and center bone intact; sometimes found skinned with bone intact.

CHILI
ancho mild, dried chilles commonly used in Mexican cooking.
chipotle pronounced cheh-pote-lay. The name used for jalapeño chilies once they've been dried and smoked. Having a deep, intensely smoky flavor, rather than a searing heat, chipotles are dark brown, almost black in colour and wrinkled in appearance.
jalapeño pronounced hah-lah-pain-yo. Fairly hot, medium-sized, plump, dark green chili; available pickled, sold canned or bottled, and fresh, from greengrocers.
long red available both fresh and dried; a generic term used for any moderately hot, long, thin chili (about 2½ in or 3 in long).
pasilla medium hot, dried chilies; could substitute ground chili powder.

red thai (serrano) also called "scuds"; tiny, very hot and bright red.

CHOCOLATE, SEMI-SWEET

also known as semi-sweet or luxury chocolate; made of a high percentage of cocoa liquor and cocoa butter, and little added sugar. Unless stated otherwise, we use dark eating chocolate in this book as it's ideal for use in desserts and cakes.

CHORIZO sausage of Spanish origin, made of coarsely ground pork and highly seasoned with garlic and chili. They are deeply smoked, very spicy and dry-cured so that they do not need cooking. Also available raw (fresh).

CILANTRO also called pak chee or chinese parsley; bright-green-leafed herb with both pungent aroma and taste. Coriander seeds are dried and sold either whole or ground, and neither tastes remotely like the fresh leaf, so should not be substituted.

CINNAMON available both in the piece (called sticks or quills) and ground into powder; one of the world's most common spices.

CLOVES dried flower buds of a tropical tree; can be used whole or in ground form. They have a strong scent and taste so should be used sparingly.

COCONUT, SHREDDED

unsweetened thin strips of dried coconut flesh.

CORNSTARCH made from wheat or 100% corn.

CREAM

heavy a whipping cream containing a thickener. Minimum fat content 35%.
pouring also called fresh or pure cream; contains no additives and

has a minimum fat content 35%.
sour a thick, commercially cultured sour cream with a minimum fat content of 35%.
thick (double) a dolloping cream with a minimum fat content of 45%.

CUCUMBER, LEBANESE short, slender and thin-skinned cucumber. Probably the most popular variety because of its tender, edible skin, tiny, yielding seeds, and sweet, fresh and flavoursome taste.

CUMIN also called zeera or comino; resembling caraway in size, cumin is the dried seed of a plant related to the parsley family. Its spicy, almost curry-like flavor is essential to the traditional foods of Mexico, India, North Africa and the Middle East. Also available ground.

EGGS we use large chicken eggs unless stated otherwise. If a recipe calls for raw or barely cooked eggs, exercise caution if there is a salmonella problem in your area, particularly in food eaten by children and pregnant women.

FLOUR

all-purpose unbleached wheat flour, making it the best for baking: the gluten content ensures a strong dough, producing a light result.
self-raising all-purpose plain or wholemeal flour with baking powder and salt added; make at home in the proportion of 1 cup flour to 2 teaspoons baking powder.

GUAVA a round or pear-shaped tropical fruit varying in size. It is thin-skinned with aromatic, sharp-sweet flesh. Varieties include strawberry guava, which is red and tastes of passionfruit and strawberries, and

cherry guava which is walnut-size. Guavas are eaten fresh and used for creamy desserts, a jelly preserve and a stiff paste to serve with cheese. Available fresh and canned.

LIQUEUR/SPIRITS

coconut-flavored we use Malibu.
orange-flavored we use Cointreau.
tequila colorless alcoholic liquor of Mexican origin made from the fermented sap of the agave, a succulent desert plant.

MUSTARD, DIJON also called french mustard. A pale brown, creamy, fairly mild mustard.

NUTMEG a strong and pungent spice. Usually available ground but the flavor is more intense from a whole nut (from spice shops), so it's best to grate your own. Often included in mixed spice mixtures.

OIL

olive made from ripened olives. Extra virgin and virgin are the first and second press, respectively, of the olives and are therefore considered the best; the "extra light" or "light" name on other types refers to taste not fat levels.
peanut pressed from ground peanuts; the most commonly used oil in Asian cooking because of its high smoke point (capacity to handle high heat without burning).
vegetable oils sourced from plant rather than animal fats.

ONION

red also known as spanish, red spanish or bermuda onion; a sweet-flavored, large, purple-red onion.
scallions also called, incorrectly, shallot; an immature onion picked before the bulb has formed, with a long, bright-green edible stalk.

PAPRIKA ground dried sweet red bell pepper; many grades and types are available, including sweet, hot, mild and smoked.

PARCHMENT PAPER or baking parchment; a silicone-coated paper used to line baking pans and oven trays so cakes and biscuits won't stick, making removal easy.

PINE NUTS also known as pignoli; not a nut but a small, cream-colored kernel from pine cones. Best roasted before use to bring out the flavor.

POLENTA also known as cornmeal; a flour-like cereal made of dried corn. Also the dish made from it.

POMEGRANATE Dark-red, leathery-skinned fresh fruit about the size of an orange. The individual cells contain seed kernels that are surrounded by an edible juice-filled sac (pulp).

RAISINS dried sweet grapes (traditionally muscatel grapes).

ROASTING/TOASTING nuts and dried coconut can be roasted in the oven to restore their fresh flavor and release aromatic oils; spread evenly onto an oven tray, roast in a moderate oven about 5 minutes. Desiccated coconut, pine nuts and sesame seeds roast more evenly if stirred over low heat in a heavy-based frying pan; their natural oils help them turn golden.

ROMAINE LETTUCE the traditional caesar salad lettuce. Long, with leaves ranging from dark green on the outside to almost white near the core; the leaves have a stiff center rib giving a slight cupping effect to the leaf on either side.

SAFFRON available in strands or ground; imparts a yellow-orange color to food once infused. Quality varies greatly; the best is the most expensive spice in the world. Store in the freezer.

SASHIMI fish sold as sashimi has to meet stringent guidelines regarding its handling. We suggest you seek local advice from authorities before eating any raw seafood.

SPINACH also known as english spinach. Baby spinach leaves are best eaten raw in salads; the larger leaves should be added last to dishes, and should be cooked until barely wilted.

STAR ANISE a dried star-shaped pod whose seeds have an astringent aniseed flavor; commonly used to flavour stocks and marinades.

SUGAR
dark brown a moist, dark brown sugar with a rich, distinctive, full flavor coming from natural molasses syrup.
light brown a very soft, finely granulated sugar retaining molasses for its characteristic color and flavor.
palm also called nam tan pip, jaggery, jawa or gula melaka; made from the sap of the sugar palm tree. Light brown to black in color and usually sold in rock-hard cakes; substitute with brown sugar.
raw natural brown granulated sugar.
superfine finely granulated table sugar.

SWISS CHARD also known, incorrectly, as spinach; has fleshy stalks and large leaves, both of which can be prepared as for spinach.

TACO SEASONING MIX packaged seasoning meant to duplicate the mild Mexican sauce made from oregano, cumin, chillies and other spices.

TOMATILLO also called a Mexican green or husk tomato. The fruit looks like a small green tomato covered in a papery husk; it has a thin, bright green skin and a tart, lemony-herb flavour. Tomatillos can ripen to yellow but are generally used while still green and quite firm.

TOMATOES
bottled pasta sauce a prepared tomato-based sauce (sometimes called ragu or sugo on the label); comes in varying degrees of thickness and levels of spicing.
canned whole peeled tomatoes in natural juices; available crushed, chopped or diced. Use undrained.
egg (plum) also called roma; smallish, oval-shaped tomatoes.
paste triple-concentrated tomato puree.

TORTILLA thin, round unleavened bread originating in Mexico; available frozen, fresh or vacuum-packed. Two kinds of tortilla are available, one made from wheat flour and the other from corn.

TURMERIC also called kamin; is a rhizome related to galangal and ginger. Must be grated or pounded to release its acrid aroma and pungent flavour; known for the golden color it imparts. Ground turmeric can be substituted for the less common fresh turmeric.

VANILLA EXTRACT made by extracting the flavour from the vanilla bean pod; pods are soaked, usually in alcohol, to capture the authentic flavor.

WATERCRESS a slightly peppery, dark-green leafy vegetable. Highly perishable, so must be used as soon as possible after purchase.

WORCESTERSHIRE SAUCE a dark colored thin condiment made from garlic, soy sauce, tamarind, onions, molasses, lime, anchovies, vinegar and seasonings. Available in supermarkets.

ZUCCHINI also known as courgette; small, pale- or dark-green, yellow or white vegetable belonging to the squash family. Harvested when young, its edible flowers can be stuffed with a then deep-fried or oven-baked.

CONVERSION CHART

MEASURES

The difference between one country's measuring cups and another's is within a two- or three-teaspoon variance, and will not affect your cooking results. North America, New Zealand and the United Kingdom use a 15ml tablespoon.

All cup and spoon measurements are level. The most accurate way of measuring dry ingredients is to weigh them. When measuring liquids, use a clear glass or plastic jug with the metric markings.

We use large eggs with an average weight of 2oz.

DRY MEASURES

IMPERIAL	METRIC
½oz	15g
1oz	30g
2oz	60g
3oz	90g
4oz (¼lb)	125g
5oz	155g
6oz	185g
7oz	220g
8oz (½lb)	250g
9oz	280g
10oz	315g
11oz	345g
12oz (¾lb)	375g
13oz	410g
14oz	440g
15oz	470g
16oz (1lb)	500g
24oz (1½lb)	750g
32oz (2lb)	1kg

LIQUID MEASURES

IMPERIAL	METRIC
1 fluid oz	30ml
2 fluid oz	60ml
3 fluid oz	100ml
4 fluid oz	125ml
5 fluid oz	150ml
6 fluid oz	190ml
8 fluid oz	250ml
10 fluid oz	300ml
16 fluid oz	500ml
20 fluid oz	600ml
1¾ pints	1000ml (1 litre)

LENGTH MEASURES

IMPERIAL	METRIC
⅛in	3mm
¼in	6mm
½in	1cm
¾in	2cm
1in	2.5cm
2in	5cm
2½in	6cm
3in	8cm
4in	10cm
5in	13cm
6in	15cm
7in	18cm
8in	20cm
9in	22cm
10in	25cm
11in	28cm
12in (1ft)	30cm

OVEN TEMPERATURES

The oven temperatures in this book are for conventional ovens; if you have a fan-forced oven, decrease the temperature by 10–20 degrees.

	°F (FAHRENHEIT)	°C (CELSIUS)
Very slow	250	120
Slow	300	150
Moderately slow	325	160
Moderate	350	180
Moderately hot	400	200
Hot	425	220
Very hot	475	240

The imperial measurements used in these recipes are approximate only. Measurements for cake pans are approximate only. Using same-shaped cake pans of a similar size should not affect the outcome of your baking. We measure the inside top of the cake pan to determine sizes.

INDEX

A

albondigas 56
aniseed sugar 120
avocado cream 26, 37

B

bananas, grilled, with coconut
    syrup 110
beans
    bean nachos 25
    black bean and mango salsa 104
    black bean, corn and
        chipotle stew 79
    chili con carne 58
    chili lamb roasts with
        black bean salad 66
    drunken 97
    red beans and rice 94
    refried 93
    shredded pork and bean soup 12
    spiced grilled beef with
        chili beans 65
beef
    albondigas 56
    blackened steak salad 57
    burritos 42
    chili con carne 58
    chipotle beef tostaditas 15
    spiced grilled beef with
        chili beans 65
black bean and mango salsa 104
black bean, corn and
    chipotle stew 79
blood orange margarita 8
burritos
    beef 42
    fish 34

C

caesar dressing 29
caesar salad, classic 29
ceviche 18

cheese
    corn and goat's cheese
        quesadillas 61
    pork and cheese quesadillas 43
chicken
    almond pomegranate sauce,
        in 55
    chicken quesadillas with
        guacamole 84
    enchiladas 44
    marinated chilli chickens 51
    mole 48
    pumpkin seed and tomatillo
        sauce, in 52
    spicy chicken tacos 80
chili chickens, marinated 51
chili con carne 58
chili con queso 19
chili lamb roasts with black
    bean salad 66
chili marinade 66
chimichangas
    coconut and pineapple 115
    shredded pork 21
chipotle beef tostaditas 15
churros 120
cinnamon syrup 112
coconut and pineapple
    chimichangas 115
cookies, mexican wedding 116
coriander sauce 76–7
corn
    barbecued corn with chunky
        salsa and rice 74
    black bean, corn and
        chipotle stew 79
    char-grilled scallops with
        corn salsa 41
    chilli seared tuna with avocado
        cream and grilled corn 37
    corn and goat's cheese
        quesadillas 61
    grilled corn and zucchini
        salsa 102
crab tostadas 26

D

dressing
    caesar 29
    lime 41
    lime buttermilk 34
    orange and dill 38
    sweet chilli 104
drinks
    blood orange margarita 8
    frozen margarita 7
    margarita 6
    mexican coffee 11
    mexican hot chocolate 10
    sangrita 9
drunken beans 97

E

eggs
    pork, olive and egg
        empanadas 24
    royal 112
    scrambled with fresh
        tomato salsa 30
empanadas, pork, olive and egg 24
enchiladas, chicken 44

F

fajitas, lamb 69
fish burritos 34
flan de cafe 108
fried sweet pastries 111
frozen margarita 7

G

green rice 96
guacamole 69, 84, 105
guavas, poached, in spicy syrup 117

H

hot sauce 100

L

lamb
    chili lamb roasts with black
      bean salad 66
    fajitas 69
    lamb shanks in chili sauce 62
lime buttermilk dressing 34
lime dressing 41

M

mango and avocado salsa 101
margarita 6
    blood orange 8
    frozen 7
mexican coffee 11
mexican hot chocolate 10
mexican rice 92
mexican wedding cookies 116
mushroom crêpes with
    coriander sauce 76–7

N

nachos, bean 25

O

orange
    blood orange margarita 8
    icing 119
    orange and dill dressing 38
oysters, fried, with salsa 16

P

paprika and parmesan polenta with
    walnut and bell pepper salsa 83
pork
    pork and cheese quesadillas 43
    pork, olive and egg
      empanadas 24
    pork ribs with chorizo and
      smoked paprika 87
    seasoned roast pork with
      prune sauce 72–3

(*pork continued*)
    shredded pork and bean soup 12
    shredded pork chimichanga 21
prune sauce 72

Q

quesadillas
    chicken quesadillas with
      guacamole 84
    corn and goat's cheese 61
    pork and cheese 43

R

red beans and rice 94
refried beans 93
rice
    barbecued corn with chunky
      salsa and rice 74
    green 96
    mexican 92
    red beans and 94
    saffron rice with zucchini
      flowers 90
royal eggs 112

S

saffron rice with zucchini flowers 90
salad
    blackened steak salad 57
    chili lamb roasts with
      black bean salad 66
    classic caesar 29
    salmon ceviche 38
salmon ceviche salad 38
salsa
    black bean and mango 104
    chunky 74
    cruda 69
    fresca 79
    fresh tomato 30
    grilled corn and zucchini 102
    mango and avocado 101
    walnut and bell pepper 83
salt cod with roasted tomatoes 47

sangrita 9
sauce
    cilantro 76–7
    hot 100
    prune 72–3
scallops
    char-grilled scallops with
      corn salsa 41
seafood
    ceviche 18
    char-grilled scallops with
      corn salsa 41
    chili seared tuna with avocado
      cream and grilled corn 37
    crab tostadas 26
    fish burritos 34
    fried oysters with salsa 16
    salmon ceviche salad 38
    salt cod with roasted tomatoes 47
    snapper veracruz 81
seasoning 72–3
snapper veracruz 81
soup
    shredded pork and bean 12
    tortilla lime 22
spiced grilled beef with
    chili beans 65
spicy chicken tacos 80
strawberry and peach tequila
    popsicles 121
sugar syrup 6, 7
sweet chili dressing 104
sweet pastries, fried 111

T

tacos, spicy chicken 80
three king bread 119
tomato salsa, fresh 30
tortilla lime soup 22
tostadas, crab 26
tostaditas, chipotle beef 15

W

walnut and bell pepper salsa 83

STERLING
New York

An Imprint of Sterling Publishing
387 Park Avenue South
New York, NY 10016

ISBN 978-1-4549-1020-6

Distributed in Canada by Sterling Publishing
c/o Canadian Manda Group, 165 Dufferin Street
Toronto, Ontario, Canada M6K 3H6

For information about custom editions, special sales, and premium and corporate purchases,
please contact Sterling Special Sales at 800-805-5489 or specialsales@sterlingpublishing.com.

Manufactured in the China

2 4 6 8 10 9 7 5 3 1

www.sterlingpublishing.com